MW01071608

Where to Watch Birds in Nicaragua

Norine –

We look forward To sharing
The birds and birding hotspots
of Nicaragua with you.

Bill Volhut
Oct 2019

Where to Watch Birds in Nicaragua

by Bill Volkert

Copyright © 2014 by William K. Volkert

ISBN: 978-1-886284-85-2

Published by
Chandler House Press, Inc.
PO Box 20126
West Side Station
Worcester, MA 01602
508-753-7419
Chandlerhousebooks.com
chandlerhousepress@yahoo.com

All rights reserved. No part of this book may be used or reproduced by any means, graphic, electronic, or mechanical, including photocopying, recording, taping or by any information storage retrieval system without the written permission of the publisher except in the case of brief quotations embodied in critical articles and reviews.

A portion of the profits from this book will go towards supporting bird conservation projects in Nicaragua.

Dedication

This book is dedicated to my wife, Connie, who has traveled across Nicaragua with me to enjoy its bird life and wonderful natural places. She has been my travel partner for the past 30 years and together we have watched birds from the Canadian Arctic to Siberia and Mongolia and from the tropics of the Americas to Africa, Australia and New Zealand.

Throughout this writing endeavor, she also has encouraged my efforts to gather the necessary information for this book and the work it took to complete it.

All text, photos and maps by Bill Volkert.

Contents

PART 2

Table of Maps

Preface

I first traveled to Nicaragua in 2002 to assist in conducting a strategic planning workshop at the Mombacho Volcano Natural Reserve. We lived at the biological station, located on top of the volcano, for nearly a week's time, leaving only to visit area schools and meet with teachers to discuss the extent or lack of conservation education in the school system. We also spent one morning birdwatching in the coffee plantation on the lower slopes of the volcano. Otherwise, the remainder of the time was spent working in the biological station or occasionally taking breaks on the trails among the cool and foggy weather of the cloud forest.

For the workshop, I joined two North Americans working in conservation education, an ornithologist from Colombia, and nine professionals from Nicaragua. This project brought together, for the first time, the ornithologists and environmental educators of Nicaragua in an effort to facilitate the development of a National Bird Conservation Education Plan.

Following this initial experience, I returned to Nicaragua 7 more times over the years. I continue to maintain contact with many of those involved in the original workshop and work with several of them to help support wildlife conservation and education programs in the country. It was as a result of these travels that I was able to experience some of the wonderful birds and birding sites throughout the country.

In writing this book I wish to share with others the birding experiences I have had in Nicaragua and encourage birders to visit Nicaragua. I also wish to support the ecotourism efforts developing in Nicaragua and hope this will encourage them to protect their wild places and natural heritage.

For those wishing to bird Nicaragua there are currently several constraints, but continued developments in ecotourism services and infrastructure are improving the ease of travel. There also is no field guide exclusively focusing on the birds of Nicaragua available at this time, though one has been in development for several years. And finally, there is also a lack of information about where to find birds, how to get there, and what species occur at specific sites.

The purpose of the book is to facilitate the independent birder to travel around Nicaragua and observe many of its birds in the diverse regions where they occur. It is hoped that by developing a bird finding guide for the country that this publication will encourage birders to explore the undiscovered land that is Nicaragua.

I have relied on numerous friends and local experts for information and bird lists for each of the sites in this book. I have made every possible effort to check each of these and verify the material. While many others have helped me in countless ways by providing the essential data about each site, I take full responsibility for its accuracy and completeness.

Acknowledgements

First of all, I wish to thank my Nicaraguan friends and colleagues who helped me in many ways with this publication. Jose Manuel Zolotoff provided critical input and review of the material contained in this book and without his assistance this publication would not have been entirely accurate and certainly not comprehensive. Likewise, I wish to thank Salvadora Morales for her input and particularly for her contribution to the information on Ometepe Island, where she is the foremost expert on the bird populations of this magical island.

Participants in the Bird Conservation Education Workshop (left to right); back row Jorge Botero, Bill Volkert, Jose Manuel Zolotoff, Sue Bonfield, Salvadora Morales, Maria Ignacia Galeano, Alexandra Zamora and Edgar Castenda. Front row: Juan Carlos Martinez Sanchez, Alejandra Martinez, Marisol Mena, Maria Jacinta Hernandez and Susan Gilchrist.

Also, my thanks to Juan Carlos Martinez Sanchez for his encouragement and review of the text. Additionally, I want to thank Georges Durieux and Lilliana Chavarria, owners and operators of El Jaguar Reserve who shared their insights on bird populations and ongoing surveys to expand our understanding of bird populations in Nicaragua.

I also want to thank Susan Gilchrist who originally invited me to participate in the Bird Conservation Education Workshop and introduced me to Nicaragua. My thanks also go to Sue Bonfield, coordinator for the North American International Migratory Bird Day program and Jorge Botero, wildlife researcher in Colombia, for their participation and contributions to this workshop. Finally, I would like to acknowledge the Nicaraguan specialists who developed their Bird Conservation Education Plan and continue to carry out the work of environmental protection, conservation education and wildlife research in the country.

The team members of the Bird Conservation Education Workshop are pictured. Additional thanks are due to the following individuals who provided critical information for the various reserves.

- Mausi Kuhl and Don Sloth of Selva Negra Reserve.
- Juan Rodriguez of Montibelli Reserve.
- Stefan Biramji, Turalu Brady Murdock and Jane Furchgott for information about Chacocente Reserve.
- Oscar Bermúdez of Los Guatuzos Reserve.and Veronica Pfanger of Greenfields Reserve.

Turquoise-browed Motmot (Guardabarranco)
Nicaragua's National Bird.

Introduction

Nicaragua is the largest country in Central America and is characterized by a prominent series of volcanoes and two vast inland lakes. It is about the size of Wisconsin with a population of 5.6 million people. Its capitol is Managua, which has a population of approximately one million. It is among the poorest countries in Central America, but the people are very friendly and hospitable.

Known for its difficult history, the Sandinista-Contra war is today all but forgotten and the country is rebuilding itself. Tourism is one of the priority ndustries that has been identified for development and birders have an opportunity to contribute to both this effort and the necessary conservation efforts to protect the natural resources of this country.

Although it has no high mountains, the northern region contains the highest elevations with cloud forest remnants and oak-pine forests. While much of the dry forest region has been converted to agriculture and other uses, there remain vast areas of undeveloped forest that support a rich diversity of wildlife. Conservation efforts have lagged behind other countries, but many of the volcanic slopes have received protection and much of the Atlantic lowland retains extensive intact tropical forest. This is largely due to the lack of roads and access that has protected this area, but also limits opportunities for visitors to only a few of the most accessible site without extensive effort.

A thorough understanding of Nicaragua's bird populations is still evolving as more organized surveys are conducted in remote areas. Protection of important conservation areas is also developing through both public and private efforts. Access to some sites is quite limited due to a lack of trails and accommodations, but increasing interest among tourists is encouraging these developments. This book focuses on many of the better developed sites in the country, and as time goes on, others will certainly be designated and some existing sites will likely become more accessible to travelers and birders alike.

Throughout Nicaragua there are many sites that provide important habitat for birds and are essential to conservation of the region's biodiversity. However, this is not a guide to all of the country's birding sites, but rather an overview of some of the most accessible and important sites representing all of the major ecoregions. It also represents those sites that I am most familiar with and was able to gather the essential information to include in this book.

Traveling in Nicaragua

Most of the towns in Nicaragua are served by buses, and directions to the birding sites by public transportation are provided for most of the sites. The local buses can at times be quite crowded and uncomfortable, but they are a reliable means of travel for those on a budget.

For the independent birder, the best way to tour the country is by car, which allows one to stop and observe birds along the way and undertake a variety of side trips to explore various areas. Rentals are available in Managua, as well as Granada and a few other large cities. However, for a wide selection of rental companies and available vehicles to choose from, making arrangements with any of the rental companies located at Sandino International Airport in Managua is recommended. This is also the most convenient for arriving international travelers.

Obviously, caution is advised when driving in Nicaragua as in any other country. In recent years the government has made large investments in road construction and in the past 5 years most of the major highways have been greatly improved. Overall, drivers are rather "civilized" and usually will yield the right-of-way, unlike some other Latin American countries where driving is more aggressive or competitive.

However, drivers need to watch for speed bumps, even on major highways, and dips constructed for drainage and run-off. Speed bumps are almost always found at school zones and usually at the city limits to designate speed zones. They are sometimes painted yellow, but many have faded over the years and others are not painted at all, so these can seem to suddenly come out of nowhere.

Driving in Managua can be very congested during rush hour, so plan accordingly. The use of GPS navigation system maps is being undertaken in many countries around the world and, while this has been available in Costa Rica for several years, it currently is very limited in Nicaragua and of little use at the time of publication of this book. It is expected that GPS systems will eventually become more widespread, which would be worthwhile even just for a trip through Managua.

While the main highways have been improved, many of the back roads are poorly maintained, and drivers need to watch for potholes and other road hazards. As a result, there is often a rather freestyle driving manner among the locals with the tendency to weave around traffic and potholes. Even on the main roads you will need to contend with numerous pedestrians, as well as bicycles, horses, and oxcarts. Therefore, driving is not recommended for the inexperienced, but in Nicaragua this isn't much different than in most other Latin American countries.

It is strongly recommended to not drive at night, particularly in rural areas. Some people like to drive without headlights, adding to the normal challenges of driving here during the daytime. Also, beware that drivers may be stopped by police for any number of supposed driving violations. They will try to keep your driver's license until you have paid the $10.00 or $15.00 fine, which is nothing more than a bribe for the local police.

Overall, driving is not considered dangerous in Nicaragua, but you need to be wary of rapidly changing road conditions, speed bumps, potholes, and congestion in the cities. For the independent birder, however, having your own vehicle has numerous advantages over other means of transportation, and site information is provided to help you find your own way to these areas.

Main highways are marked in kilometers (usually indicating the distance from Managua) with concrete markers along the roadside. Directions to birding sites often indicate at which kilometer (km) to turn onto another road. Distances along side roads to sites are given in kilometers.

Climate and Timing

Nicaragua is largely a low lying country with warm to hot tropical temperatures. Annual variations occur between the wet and dry seasons with the driest months being February through April. The Pacific coast is warmer but drier than the Atlantic coast, and the highlands of the north provide the most comfortable temperatures. During the rainy season many of the roads can be difficult to travel and four-wheel drive will be required to reach many locations.

Accommodations

There are adequate to fine accommodations in all of the larger cities and many of the sites listed in this book provide lodging on the grounds of the reserve. However, eco-lodges are still developing in Nicaragua and therefore remain quite limited.

Overall, prices are low by American standards, although costs rise at the larger hotels in the major cities. Prices given here are based on the most recent information available from each of the sites. These will change over time and therefore are offered as a general estimate. Prices are given in U.S. dollars and Nicaraguan Cordobas (C$), which has been going at an exchange rate of about 25 to one.

Camping is available at a few of the reserves and is necessary in the most remote sites. However, affordable housing is available at numerous locations nearby or within most of the reserves featured in this book.

Food, Health and Safety

In all hot tropical countries there is a risk of food contamination, so use common sense when eating meats, fruits, and vegetables. With recent improvements to the local tourism economy and more reliable power production, refrigeration is becoming more common and widespread, enhancing food safety. Travelers should have inoculations against hepatitis A and typhoid, and if traveling in the eastern lowlands you should consider precautions against malaria. Also, dengue fever is present, particularly in low-lying areas. The best precaution for either of these mosquito-bourne diseases is prevention through proper clothing and use of repellent. Check with the Center for Disease Control for current information and recommended vaccinations.

Other potential hazards include bees and wasps, especially for those with allergic reactions, and scorpions. It is a good practice to keep your bags or suitcases closed and to check your shoes before putting them on. More of a nuisance than a danger is chiggers. They tend to live in dried grass, leaves and open fields. Avoid these areas if possible, or tuck your pants into your socks and use repellent if walking there.

Nicaragua does have several species of poisonous snakes. However, these are rarely encountered by most visitors. The best advice is to stay on marked trails and watch where you put your feet if you get off of designated trails.

Much of the country has a very low crime rate and is quite safe for foreigners, but common sense is warranted in the larger cities. The greatest risk comes from crimes of opportunity rather than violent crime. Check the U.S. State Department Travel Advisories for recent updates.

One consideration is to purchase a disposable cell phone, which is available at kiosks in the larger cities. Minutes can be purchased at numerous sites throughout the country. With the development of cell phone service in the country, communication is rapidly improving and this can be helpful along the way and aid in case of emergency.

Time Zone and Language

Nicaragua is located in the Central Standard Time Zone or GMT minus six hours. Nicaragua does not observe daylight saving time, but for travelers from the United States there is little to no change in time.

Spanish is the official language of Nicaragua, as in nearly all Latin American countries. Some familiarity with the language is certainly recommended, but for those with limited to no knowledge of Spanish you can still get around Nicaragua. English is increasingly being recognized by many Nicaraguans as a very useful and marketable skill and opens vast opportunities to those who have the desire and chance to learn it. As a result, many younger people are trying to learn English as a second language and are often eager to practice their skills.

At most all of the larger hotels and many restaurants in the larger cities, staff will speak some English. At most establishments in smaller towns and in the countryside there will be few if any people familiar with English. Many of the established lodges employ at least one person that speaks some English.

Local Currency and Exchange Rates

The local currency is the Cordoba (indicated as C$), originally named for the Spanish explorer, Francisco Hernández de Córdoba. In early 2013 the exchange rate was 24 to one against U.S. dollars. Some prices given in the book are rounded off due to fluctuating exchange rates since the information was first obtained.

If you fail to exchange dollars when you arrive, you will find that dollars are readily accepted throughout the country. It is not advised to take traveler's cheques or try to conduct business at the local banks for the simple fact that this can be a lengthy process for those in a hurry to do some birding.

Your best bet for obtaining dollars or cordobas is to use the ATM's, which can be found at the banks in any major city. I have experienced problems with some of these machines not accepting certain cards or often times limiting the amount of withdrawals to only $100 or $200 dollars, or the equivalent in cordobas, at a time. When using an ATM card, try a major bank to be sure it works and then try to stay with these machines throughout your trip. Remember, if you do experience problems with your card, only try this twice in a day so that you won't have your card locked out by security procedures. This can be difficult and very inconvenient to rectify when in a foreign country.

Electricity and Phone Service

For those traveling with electric powered or electronic equipment with rechargers for laptops and digital cameras, Nicaragua runs on 110 volt, two-prong outlets. This is the same as in the U.S., so there is no need for power or outlet converters for travelers from North America.

Power generation in the country has become much more reliable in recent years and the country experiences fewer rolling blackouts than in the past. Those concerned with their electronics may want to bring a surge protector, although this appears to be no more of a problem here than elsewhere.

Internet cafes and Wifi service are rapidly becoming widespread and should be available at most hotels in the larger cities and other establishments. Likewise, cell phone service is becoming available across much of Nicaragua, and even in some more remote areas, phone service is now available.

If you are calling from out of the country, Nicaragua's country code is 505. For those driving long distances in the country, purchase of a cell phone at any of the kiosks at the airport or larger stores is suggested. The current cell phone providers in Nicaragua are Movistar and Claro.

Birdwatching in Nicaragua

While birding and nature-based tourism are well established in Costa Rica, Nicaragua is still a frontier. However, it offers great opportunities for nature-based tourism and provides birders the chance to add to our understanding of bird populations in this country. Birding in Nicaragua is not that popular among the general public and is still developing as a form of tourism. However, birding is becoming more recognized among those promoting tourism, and native wildlife has been identified as one of the major potential ecotourism attractions, which also can encourage and support local conservation efforts.

The development of birdwatching as a tourist attraction can also support the protection of natural reserves and important ecological habitats, if developed properly. Other benefits of ecotourism may include job creation for guides and park rangers, as well as the service industry to

assist and provide for tourists. It can also encourage a greater environmental awareness among local communities, which can help protect vital habitats and support conservation efforts.

To date, a total of 749 species of birds have been recorded in Nicaragua. This list continues to grow as a result of more thorough surveys throughout the country and in remote areas. In 2000, there were 644 species known to occur in Nicaragua. More recently a comprehensive checklist of birds (2007, Martinez, et. al) cited 708 species, and several new species have been discovered since then.

Therefore, there is tremendous opportunity for birders to add to our understanding of the birds of Nicaragua by documenting and sharing their sightings. Nicaragua truly is an unexplored land for birders and researchers alike. Of course, the great variety of birds to be found here demonstrates the rich diversity of habitats in the country.

A percentage of Nicaragua's birds are North American migrants, being present for only part of the year. These neotropical migrants may spend the entire northern winter in Nicaragua, or they may pass through the country enroute to wintering sites located farther south. Generally, migrants can be observed in Nicaragua from about September to April.

A great number of resident species can be seen at any time of year and birding opportunities exist throughout Nicaragua. While some of the richest sites, such as the Indio Maiz Biological Reserve, will require extra effort to reach, many great birding sites are readily accessible.

The focus of this book is to highlight a range of sites that represent the diverse biogeographical areas and habitats in Nicaragua and to emphasize those sites that tend to be most accessible. While many other protected areas exist in the country, they are not easy to access, and I did not obtain sufficient information to fully include them in this publication.

The unique geographic location of Nicaragua provides this Central American country with some special assets. Nicaragua contains the largest inland lakes and largest protected area in Central America. From oak-pine forest and cloud forest remnants in the Northern Highlands to the vast Caribbean lowlands, the diverse ecoregions of Nicaragua provide essential habitat to a wide range of bird species.

Species Names and Checklists

Birds are listed throughout the book by their common English name, which most North American birders rely on, and is how they are commonly first cited in field guides and checklists. Common names for the species are capitalized throughout the book for emphasis. A complete checklist with common and scientific names can be found in the appendix.

Common and scientific names for bird species follow the 6th Edition of the Clement's Checklist of Birds of the World (2011). As a result of recent revisions to the world checklist, several of the bird species known to Nicaragua have seen changes to their scientific and/or common names. Therefore, some field guides and references will differ in the names of species cited.

Recent changes to common names of Nicaraguan birds include:

Scaled Dove	Inca Dove
Fork-tailed Emerald	Cavinet's Emerald
Chestnut-mandibled Toucan	Black-mandibled Toucan
Violaceous Trogon	Gartered Trogon
Straight-billed Gnatwren	Long-billed Gnatwren
Yellow-throated Brush-Finch	White-naped Brush-Finch

There have also been several splits among species. For example, Green Parakeet is now Green and Pacific Parakeet, and others are expected.

Among various field guides and checklists, the order and grouping of numerous species have changed with recent revisions; some quite radically. This may result in some searching to find the species by common or scientific name among different versions of checklists. Examples include the splitting of tanagers between true tanagers and Piranga tanagers, which are now grouped with the cardinals; seedeaters, seed-finches, and saltators are grouped with true tanagers; and euphonias have been moved to the cardueline finches. However, as most birders can understand, this is a never-ending process as our understanding of birds increases and is also the nature of keeping a checklist or life list.

The checklist in the appendix was adapted from Lista Patron De Las Aves De Nicaragua (The Checklist of the Birds of Nicaragua) by Juan Carlos Martinez-Sanchez, et.al, 2007. A few recent additions to this list have been included from various sources. For both the complete checklist in the appendix and the many site lists of bird species, I have followed the most recent order in Clements (2011). Those wishing to share their sightings and document uncommon or new species for Nicaragua are encouraged to submit these to eBird Central America at http://ebird.org/content/camerica/ and/or www.nicabirds.com.

The species lists that have been included for the featured sites come from a variety of sources. I have tried to include a fairly detailed list for each of the sites to the extent that these were available. These lists are not entirely complete, due to lists being continuously updated, and since I chose not to list the most obvious species, such as Turkey and Black Vulture, Tropical Kingbird, Social Flycatcher, Great-tailed Grackle, House Sparrow among a few others. If you are looking for birds while traveling in Nicaragua you should find these almost everywhere.

The objective of these property lists is to provide a summary of the wide range of representative species at the site, including those likely to be sighted as well as less common species of particular interest to birders. Those species that are best found at these sites or assumed target species for most birders are given in the section of specialties. This is, of course, very subjective and each birder will have his own idea of specialties.

Site Names and Measurements

The various birding sites are first listed by their English name followed by their Spanish name, given in italics, to aid in travel in the country. Distances are provided in kilometers, because roads are measured in kilometers, and all rental cars have odometers and speedometers in metric units.

Measurements are given in hectares for nearly all of the sites, as most of the available information was provided in these units, followed by acres (a hectare of land is about 2.5 acres). Elevations are given in meters, followed by feet, again due to information being available as such with conversions for the convenience of a North American audience.

Site Maps

The maps in this book were developed by the author and were derived from a variety of sources, including brochures and publications from many of the reserves, as well as other cartographic sources. There is no scale of distances included with the maps since they vary in scale from one map to the next. It is expected that travelers will have access to a road map of Nicaragua for reference. The intended purpose of the maps in this book is primarily to show the relative location of the different sites and to indicate the best travel route to reach them.

Bird Diversity

Nicaragua supports 74 families of birds and nearly 750 species. This list is certain to grow as additional surveys and research add to the known variety of birds in the country. Nicaragua does not contain any true endemics, but it is the best place in Central America to observe Green-breasted Mountain-gem and Nicaraguan Grackle, which are near-endemics. Also, the Nicaraguan Seed-Finch is only found from Nicaragua to western Panama.

Due to Nicaragua's location, the country forms the northernmost or southernmost limit for several species of birds. For example, the Yellow-winged Tanager, Green-breasted Mountain-gem and Common Raven reach their southern limit in the Northern Highlands of Nicaragua. Also, another hummingbird species, the Purple-throated Mountain-gem, does not occur north of Nicaragua.

Geography and Bird Habitats of Nicaragua

Nicaragua's varied geography provides the foundation for a wide variety of vegetative communities and wildlife habitats. This is the "Land of Volcanoes", with a string of prominent cinder cones that stand in a line along the length of the country accenting the landscape. Located in the region of dry tropical forest, their higher elevations are covered in dense forest and cloud forest on some of the peaks.

In broad general terms, Nicaragua can be divided into three major regions as described by Taylor (1963); the Pacific Region, Central Highlands, and Atlantic Lowlands. Within these regions are a range of different ecosystems, including tropical dry forests, cloud forests, rainforests (also referred to as wet tropical forests), mangroves, wetlands, and savannas. Different naturalists have used various methods to classify the diverse natural communities in the tropics. I have chosen to rely on broad habitat descriptions as an aid to non-professionals and the general birding public.

The Atlantic Lowlands are dominated by dense, humid tropical forests and cover extensive areas of Nicaragua. The Northern Highlands are defined by low mountains and plateaus with forests of pine and oak on the drier slopes and cloud forest remnants in the higher elevations.

The western part of the country is primarily tropical dry forest and scrub, with farmland and many towns and cities. This is where the majority of the people live. This region is characterized by a series of volcanoes that run nearly the length of the country and contains the two large water bodies of Lake Managua and Lake Nicaragua.

The western part of Nicaragua is bordered by the Pacific Ocean, which marks the edge of the dry forest and surrounding farmland. These deciduous forests have been fragmented by farming and extend down to the sand-washed coast and mangrove forests. To the north lies Honduras and its rolling hills, and to the south is Costa Rica where the highest mountains of Central America have formed.

The central lowlands essentially separate the Mexican and northern Central American flora and fauna from the southern Central American biome. This is why many birders visiting Nicaragua take field guides to both the birds of Mexico and Costa Rica. Much of the Atlantic lowlands and the central part of Nicaragua contain birds associated with Costa Rica and Panama, while the northern highlands contain species associated with the highlands of southern Mexico, Guatemala and Honduras. The Central American pine forests reach their southern extent in the northern highlands as do numerous bird species found there.

Tropical Wet Forest

Extensive tropical wet forest, also known as tropical rainforest, still exists in Nicaragua, particularly in the eastern lowlands. There are several big reserves in these lowlands—the Indio Maiz Biological Reserve and Guatuzos Reserve in the southeastern part of Nicaragua, and the Bosawás Biosphere Reserve in the northern part of

Nicaragua. Both areas contain expansive forests and a wide range of rainforest animals.

Tropical wet forest covers most of the eastern portion of the country in the Atlantic lowlands. Common birds of this region include Mealy Parrot, Great Green and Scarlet Macaw, White-necked Puffbird, Great Jacamar, Keel-billed Toucan, Bare-necked Umbrellabird, Purple-throated Fruitcrow, and various antbirds.

Ecoregions of Nicaragua

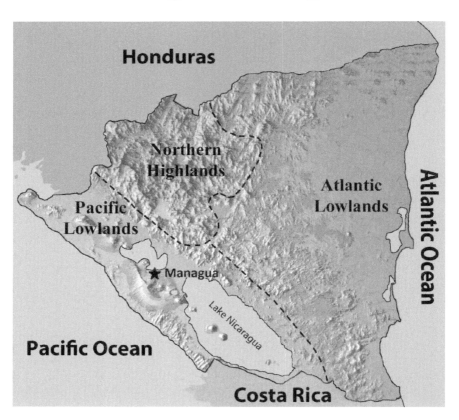

Tropical Dry Forest

In addition to rainforests, there also are tropical dry forests. This forest community is found from southern Mexico to northern Costa Rica and occurs along the Pacific side of these countries where highlands block the moist prevailing easterly winds.

Lack of rain during the dry season causes trees to shed their leaves during part of the year (roughly from February until May) in order to conserve water. During this season the forest is less densely vegetated, which aids in observing birds among the trees and shrubs. Much of this forest has been converted to farmland, and only remnants of this once extensive forest remain. Typical dry-forest birds include Lesser Ground-Cuckoo, Hoffmann's Woodpecker, Pacific Parakeet, White-throated Magpie-Jay, Rufous-naped Wren, and Long-tailed Manakin.

Semi-deciduous Forest

Another type of forest that can be found in Nicaragua is semi-deciduous tropical forest. This forest type has more rain and humidity than the dry forest, but without the permanent rainfall and humidity of wet tropical forests. As a result, many trees are able to hold their leaves throughout the year, making these forests much greener than the dry tropical forest, even during the dry season. This type of vegetation is typically found on the Pacific side at elevations from about 400 to 800 meters (1,200 to 2,500 feet). Bird species in the semi-deciduous forest are similar to those of the dry tropical forest.

Montane Forest and Cloud Forest

Found at elevations above the semi-deciduous forest is the montane forest that give way to cloud forest on the highest slopes. Cloud forest exists at elevations ranging from about 1,000 meters (3,500 feet) and above. These forests blanket the upper reaches of the tallest volcanoes, such as Mombacho Volcano and the Maderas Volcano, and also are found on the highest peaks in the Northern Highlands. These two volcanoes are the only areas with cloud forest on the Pacific side of Nicaragua.

These high peaks can be covered in clouds on most days, resulting in nearly constant high humidity. The climate supports the unique vegetation of a high elevation evergreen forest. The high humidity also allows for tremendous plant growth and productivity with a high degree of diversity where many different plant and animal species can be found in a small area. Cloud forests are often times too dense to hike through without a trail. The larger trees support epiphytes, such as orchids, bromeliads and other plants that grow on tree trunks and branches, providing great habitats for insects and food for a variety of birds.

Plants and animals living in these island habitats of cloud forests are isolated from other similar areas and this has resulted in the development of several locally endemic species. At the Mombacho Volcano, for instance, there occurs an endemic salamander, fern, shrub, and orchid.

Some particular birds of the cloud forests include Purple-throated Mountain-gem, Mountain Eleania, Slate-colored Solitaire, Black-faced and Ruddy-capped Nightingale-Thrush, Mountain Thrush, Three-wattled Bellbird, Resplendent Quetzal, and Chestnut-capped Brush-Finch.

The Mombacho Volcano is also known for another unique type of vegetation. At the summit there is a near-constant strong wind that has resulted in stunting the growth of trees and shrubs. This dense, twisted forest is known as a dwarf forest or elfin forest.

Oak-Pine Forest

Occurring on the drier granite slopes of the highlands is an unusual tropical community of oak and pines. This forest type extends from the highlands of southern Mexico to northern Nicaragua. This oak-pine forest is an open-grown forest located on mountain slopes. Several species of birds associated with this forest reach the southern extent of their range in northern Nicaragua. Some of the birds associated with the oak-pine forest include White-eared Hummingbird, Azure-crowned Hummingbird, and Greater Pewee. Recently, surveys have discovered a wintering population of the federally endangered Golden-cheeked Warbler in these forests.

Coastal Areas

The extensive coasts of the Atlantic and Pacific Oceans form long beaches and tidal wetlands. These coasts attract a wide range of waterbirds, including Magnificent Frigatebird, Brown Pelican, a variety of gulls and terns, plus herons, egrets, and spoonbills in suitable habitat. They also can be important for migrant and wintering shorebirds. Surveys have recently begun to identify shorebird stop-over habitat, particularly in the Gulf of Fonseca.

Just off the Atlantic Coast are two small islands called the Corn Islands and beyond lie the Pearl Keys. The Corn Islands are the only known site in Nicaragua for Smooth-billed Ani and White-crowned Pigeon.

To date, pelagic birds have been poorly surveyed in Nicaragua, and there are no organized pelagic birding tours available in the country. It is certain that more species will be recorded in the near-shore waters of the country as additional surveys are conducted.

Mangrove Forest and Wetlands

Mangroves are found among estuaries and coastal shorelines along the Atlantic and Pacific coasts. Roots of mangrove trees are partially submerged and provide an important aquatic habitat for organisms like oysters, barnacles, and plankton. They also support abundant fish populations that in turn provide a feeding ground for many birds.

A variety of wading birds can be found among the mangroves as well as a race of the Yellow Warbler, the Mangrove Warbler. Some of the birds of the wet tropical forest edge also are attracted to the mangroves.

Another important habitat can be found among the many kinds of wetlands. Migrant waterfowl and shorebirds can gather in large flocks in these shallow-water habitats. Several of Nicaragua's wetlands have been designated as Ramsar Sites, or "Wetlands of International Importance", such as Tisma Lagoon and Lake Apanas. These are good places to watch for over-wintering waterfowl, a variety of herons and egrets, rails, and migrant shorebirds.

Other Ecosystems

Nicaragua also contains a variety of small lakes as well as Lake Managua and Lake Nicaragua. Lake Nicaragua (also called Lago Cocibolca) is the largest lake in Central America. This lake contains an archipelago of islands called Solentiname, plus the hundreds of tiny islands (called isletas) by Granada. Solentiname harbors a tremendous nesting colony of wading birds that take advantage of the isolation of the islands for nesting and nearby wetlands for feeding.

Together, these diverse landscape features provide essential habitat for a wide array of wildlife and also define some wonderfully scenic areas across Nicaragua. A birding trip to Nicaragua will provide opportunities to observe a wide range of bird species and the chance to experience the varied landscape of this Central American country.

Field Guides

There are several useful field guides that are of help to those birding in Nicaragua, although unfortunately there presently is no exclusive Nicaraguan bird guide. They include:

- A Guide to the Birds of Mexico and Northern Central America by Howell and Webb (1995).
- The Guide to the Birds of Costa Rica by Stiles and Skutch (1989).
- The Birds of Costa Rica by Garrigues and Dean (2007).
- A Guide to the Birds of Panama by Ridgely and Gwynne (1989).

Also, see the reference section at the end of this book for additional sources of information.

Birding Sites and Routes

This book is organized by the various biogeographical regions of Nicaragua and provides information about many of the more accessible and representative sites located throughout the country. Altogether, more than two dozen sites are featured. This book has been divided into five distinct regions, representing diverse habitats and ecoregions of the country. There are six sections, with two to six featured sites per section. These sites can be visited individually or combined as a travel route to provide birding trips of a few days to a week or more in the various sectors of the country. Following this book on an extended tour of Nicaragua will lead you throughout the country with an opportunity to see the widest range of species possible.

I first focus on the easiest-to-get-to sites in the vicinity of Managua, the capitol through which nearly all visitors arrive. This is followed by a series of nearby sites accessible from Managua or Granada. From here, a series of birding routes are possible to explore the different regions and habitats of the country along the Pacific Coast, the central Lake Nicaragua area, the Atlantic Lowlands, and the Northern Highlands.

Each section begins with a regional map indicating the approximate location of the various sites covered and a brief overview of the region. This includes a description of the habitats of each ecoregion, a summary of the sites featured in each section, plus a list of additional available sites. These additional sites are briefly summarized at the end of each section following the detailed featured site information, since they are either very remote or I did not have complete information available at the time of publication to include them in detail as a featured site.

Following the regional overview, a detailed summary of each birding site is provided, containing the following information: a general description of the site, directions on how to get there, information about access fees, hours of operation if applicable, and available accommodations. There also is contact information for each site office and/or accommodations for information or reservations. For each featured birding site, maps of the property and/or trails have been included. This is followed by a description of the best birding locations on the property and a list of bird species to be found there.

The bird lists, as mentioned above, are quite extensive and as complete and accurate as possible, based on the best available information. The most common Nicaraguan bird species, found at all featured sites and throughout most or all of the country, have been excluded. The bird lists also include a separate list of specialties, which may include those species that are characteristic of a particular site and easy to find there or rare species of limited range and/or populations that have been recorded at the site.

Stripe-headed Sparrow

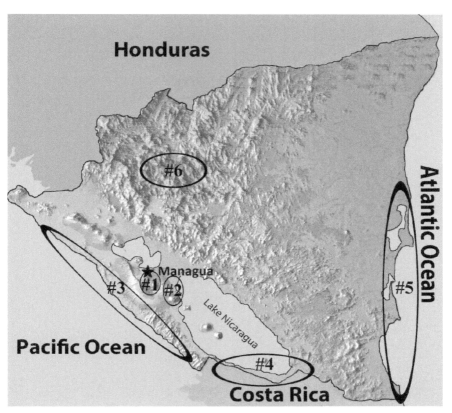

1 – Managua Area   4 – Southern Lake Nicaragua
2 – Granada Area   5 – Atlantic Lowlands
3 – Pacific Coast   6 – Northern Highlands

The Pacific Lowlands

White-throated Magpie-Jay

Region 1
The Pacific Lowlands;
The Land of Lakes and Volcanoes

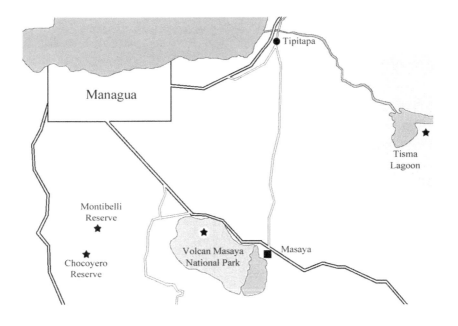

Located in a region of dry tropical forest with farms and urban areas, there are four premier birding sites readily accessible from Managua. For those with only a few days in the country, these sites are easily reached as day trips from the capitol and provide a great introduction to the birds of Nicaragua.

Managua/Masaya Area

There are several sites located near Managua that can easily be visited by those with limited time in the country or serve as starting points for longer trips. While staying in the city center will add considerably to your travel time, a range of accommodations can be found on the outskirts of Managua and in nearby towns, as well as at Montibelli Reserve. Birders will understand that staying in a city can make quite a difference when added to early morning travel in order to arrive at sites at the break of dawn.

Managua is like most capitol cities in Central and South America—it is the point of entry for most travelers and a large, busy metropolis. For a major city, it has a large amount of tree cover and as a result nearly 40 species of birds have been recorded here, providing urban birding opportunities. While the city also has a number of historic and cultural sites that can be visited, information on tourist attractions can be found in various travel guides, such as Lonely Planet or Moon Guide books.

The low mountains of the Managua Sierra, which lie south and west of the capitol, rise more than 600 meters (2,000 feet) above the surrounding lowlands. Much of this region has been designated as a biological corridor, protecting the forested hillsides as a vital watershed. These uplands also provide more moderate temperatures compared to the nearby lowlands. This range is characterized by rolling hills and steep valleys and is covered in dry tropical forest and semi-deciduous forest, while the surrounding area is dominated by farmland and cities. It is but a remnant of the once expansive dry forest that covered this entire region and today provides important habitat for a wide range of bird species.

There are several great birding sites located in this area and all are within a rather short drive from Managua. This section provides detailed information on four birding sites in the Managua/Masaya area. Both Chocoyero-El Brujo Natural Reserve and Montebilli Nature Reserve have been established within the Managua Sierra. Chocoyero Reserve lies within a steep valley and is known for its large population of Pacific Parakeets, while Montibelli is a shade-grown coffee plantation with dry tropical forest.

The Masaya Volcano is located about 30 minutes from Managua along the Managua-Masaya Highway. It is both a national park and Nicaragua's most accessible volcano. This park contains much open grassland but also protects a remnant of dry tropical forest. The nature center provides a good introduction to the geology of Nicaragua.

Tisma Lagoon and Wetland holds great potential for birds and is a Ramsar Site; a designated Wetland of International Importance. This shallow lake with its extensive surrounding wetlands can be difficult to access but is one of the few vast wetlands in this part of the country.

Several other reserves and protected areas are to be found in this region of the country, but have not been included as featured sites due to limited information. However, they can provide additional birding opportunities and a chance to further explore the country. They include Chiltepe Peninsula Natural Reserve, Monte Galan Lagoon, and Quelantaro Private Reserve. As ecotourism and conservation efforts continue to develop, other protected sites are certain to become established in this area.

Blue-gray Tanager

William Volkert

The Birds of Managua

Black Vulture
Turkey Vulture
Rock Pigeon
Red-billed Pigeon
White-winged Dove
Ruddy Ground-Dove
Inca Dove
Orange-fronted Parakeet
Orange-chinned Parakeet
Groove-billed Ani
Ferruginous Pygmy-Owl
Common Pauraque
Cinnamon Hummingbird
Turquoise-browed Motmot
Hoffmann's Woodpecker
Social Flycatcher
Great Kiskadee

Tropical Kingbird
Scissor-tailed Flycatcher
White-throated Magpie-Jay
Gray-breasted Martin
Barn Swallow
Rufous-naped Wren
Clay-colored Thrush
Yellow Warbler
Rufous-capped Warbler
Blue-gray Tanager
Grayish Saltator
Stripe-headed Sparrow
Great-tailed Grackle
Bronzed Cowbird
Spot-breasted Oriole
Streak-backed Oriole
Baltimore Oriole
House Sparrow

The ubiquitous Tropical Kingbird

Masaya Volcano National Park
(*Parque Nacional Volcan Masaya*)

Site Description:

Masaya Volcano National Park is Nicaragua's most accessible natural attraction and its premier tourist site. This is one of the few volcanoes in the world where you can drive up to the crater's edge and look down into the mouth of the crater, which is continuously emitting smoke and gases.

Masaya Volcano emits a nearly constant plume of sulfurous gas, smoke and sometimes ash, visible from as far away as the airport in Managua. From one of its craters, you can sometimes observe incandescent rock and magma. A visitor center provides information and displays on the geology and ecology of the park. Hiking trails cover a portion of the volcano's slope and surrounding dry tropical forest.

The park encompasses an area of 5,400-hectares (13,343 acres) and features several geologically-linked volcanic craters. There are actually two volcanoes and five craters located here. The volcanoes have erupted several times in recent history, and this is considered one of Nicaragua's most active volcanoes.

Volcan Nindiri last erupted in 1670, and Volcan Masaya's most legendary eruption was in 1772. Rocks and volcanic ashes still cover the area surrounding the volcanoes, and vegetation is slowly re-establishing in this area. The relatively new Santiago Crater was formed between the other two craters in 1852. It is inhabited by a population of Pacific Parakeets that nest along the crater walls in spite of the toxic gases. It is possible to see these "chocoyos del crater" (crater parakeets) from the parking area, particularly in the morning and late afternoon.

Directions:

The park lies less than 30 minutes from Managua and ten minutes from Masaya. The park is located on the Managua-Masaya Highway (Carretera Masaya) at Kilometer 23. From the entrance of the park, it is five kilometers uphill to the Masaya Volcano, located at the center of the park. Visitors can drive to the crater, or hikers can ask a taxi driver to drive there. Hiking uphill is possible, but the road is steep, and much of the road offers little shade and lacks extensive wildlife habitat.

Access/accommodations:

A well designed visitor center is located along the road leading to the volcano. The center provides information about the Masaya Volcano and also the other volcanoes in Nicaragua, plus related geological processes. Visitors can also learn more about the flora and fauna of the park.

Hours of operation:

Open every day from 9:00 am to 4:45 pm. Entrance fee is about $4.00.

Contact Information:

Phone: (505) 2528-1444   Website: http://vianica.com/attraction/2/masaya-volcano-national-park.

The Santiago Crater with its ever-present smoke.

Trails

From the parking area at the central crater, a series of hiking trails lead to other craters and overlooks. Occasionally some trails will be closed, depending on the activity of the volcano and prevailing winds that carry the sulfurous fumes. While bird habitat is limited on the open slopes, the trails do offer good views of the smoking volcano and the surroundings landscape. Daytime temperatures can become quite hot, so plan to hike early in the day.

Another trail leads to Tzinaconostoc Cave, a lava tube that houses hundreds of bats. Guided night tours begin at sunset to see the bat cave or craters. A crater opening that formed in 2006 is located deep inside the crater and can only be seen at night. The cost is $10.00 per person, with a minimum group size of 6 and a maximum of 40 people.

Unfortunately, the park does not open until mid-morning, which is not particularly accommodating to birders. However, special arrangements may be made in advance with the park staff.

30

Trails vary in distance between 1.4 and 5.9 kilometers. Each trail takes between one to four hours to complete. The longest trail, the Coyote Trail, leads to Masaya Lake (Laguna de Masaya) through the largest dry forest stand in the park. Maps are available at the visitor center, or you can sign up to participate in guided hikes, including a night hike.

Description of Birding Sites:

Birding opportunities exist in the dry forest surrounding the visitor center and along the road leading from the visitor center to the crater. This road passes through stands of dry forest, grasses, and lava fields devoid of vegetation. Stopping along here can be a problem as the road is narrow and buses and cars often travel the road to and from the crater. However, if you find a place to stop on the side of the road while keeping a view of oncoming traffic, you may be able to watch for birds from the roadside.

At the Santiago Crater, hiking trails go up the surrounding hills to adjacent craters that attract several common bird species, but much of this area is lacking in trees and shrubs due to the sulfurous gases that are emitted from the volcano. The best area for birding is the dry forest around the visitor center and along the Coyote Trail that leads to the shores of Lake Masaya. However, the lake is quite polluted and areas are inhabited by land squatters, so caution is advised near the lake.

Birds of the Area:

The primary focus of this park is the geological landscape, but it is known among birders for the Pacific Parakeets that nest and roost along the volcano walls. These birds have somehow adapted to the sulfur smoke emanating from the volcano. During the day the parakeets search for food in agricultural fields up to 20 km away, but around sunset they return to their nests. Arrival time varies from day to day depending on how far they have traveled to find food.

Other species include White-winged Dove, Common and Ruddy Ground-Dove, Hoffmann's Woodpecker, Scissor-tailed Flycatcher, White-throated Magpie-Jay, Band-backed Wren, Blue-gray Tanager, and Variable Seedeater, among other dry-forest and open field species.

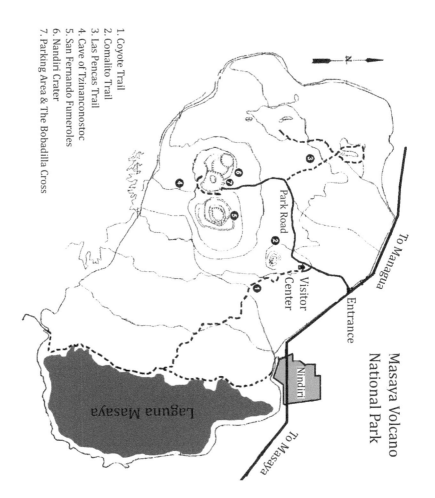

Masaya Volcano
National Park

1. Coyote Trail
2. Comalito Trail
3. Las Pencas Trail
4. Cave of Tzinanconostoc
5. San Fernando Fumeroles
6. Nandiri Crater
7. Parking Area & The Bobadilla Cross

Laguna Masaya

Nindiri

To Managua

To Masaya

Entrance

Visitor Center

Park Road

N

Chocoyero & El Brujo Wildlife Refuge
(*Refugio de Vida Silvestre Chocoyero-El Brujo*)

Site Description:

The Chocoyero-El Brujo Natural Reserve is a relatively small protected area, at 184 hectares (454 acres), but is a great place to hike and bird. This reserve is known for its Pacific Parakeets that nest and roost at a waterfall in the reserve. Called chocoyos, from which the park gets its name, the parakeets can be seen every morning around sunrise when they leave their nests, and again just before sunset when they return, just as at Masaya Volcano. However, this is a more significant population.

Chocoyero-El Brujo Reserve was included in the national protected areas in 1993 and is located less than 30 kilometers from Managua. The area is mostly dry tropical forest surrounded by volcanic ridges with semi-deciduous forest in higher elevations. At the far end of the trail is a steep cliff and waterfall. This forms a creek that flows through the lower portion of the reserve.

33

The waterfalls are small, particularly in the dry season, but worth the hike. The water comes from rain gathered further up in the mountains and is collected as drinking water for the nearby communities.

In addition to a wide variety of birds, both howler and white-face monkeys inhabit the park. The howler monkeys, locally called congos, may be heard from a great distance in the valley. These monkeys are often seen from the Congo Trail, for which the trail is named.

The reserve has several trails and also offers night-hikes and camping. Birds are easily seen from any of the trails, and guides are available to lead a hike and tell you about the reserve and its wildlife. The guides are well trained observers and can help locate birds and other wildlife. Inquire at the office for trail maps or guide services.

Directions:

To get to Chocoyero from Managua, take the main highway (Carretera Masaya) toward Masaya. It will require about one hour to drive there from Managua. Watch for the small green signs marking kilometers. At the traffic circle at Km 14.4 turn right toward Ticuantepe, then take another right at the first traffic light (3.5 kilometers farther) in the direction of San Marcos (this road is called La Concha). In another three kilometers, at Km 21.5 along Carretera Ticuantepe, you'll find a sign on the right that points to a dirt road to Chocoyero–El Brujo Reserve.

Take a sharp right as you leave the pavement and take a hairpin turn down a steep hill. Four-wheel drive is not necessary, but caution will be required in places with a sedan. However, a four wheel drive may be needed in the rainy season when the road gets muddy. From here, dirt roads wind through pineapple and banana farms. This is a good place to watch for motmots, trogons and a variety of dry forest and forest edge species. From the paved road, it is about 7 km to the park. Watch for faded signs at the intersections and stay on the well-used though narrow road, or ask locals to point the direction to the park.

It will take about 30 minutes after leaving the highway to arrive at the nature center and trail head, and roadside birding can add greatly to the drive time. Caution is advised on all dirt roads as road condition may change suddenly.

Public Transportation: The town of Ticuantepe can be easily reached from Managua and other nearby cities. From Ticuantepe, there are small buses (microbuses) that head to Los Rios, a community close to the reserve. These microbuses leave every hour between 7:00 am and 5:00 pm during the week and until 4:00 pm on weekends. The price is less than $1.00. From Los Rios, it is a three kilometer walk to the reserve. Another possibility is to take one of the red motor taxis from Ticuantepe to the reserve, which costs around C$80 ($3.00).

Access/accommodations:

As you arrive at Chocoyero Reserve, you will find a small parking area and nature center. Maps and information are available here. Special tours are also offered, including a night-hike, a bird hike with a naturalist, and adventure hikes. To make arrangements for any of these special hikes, be sure to contact the reserve beforehand.

Chocoyero also offers the opportunity of staying in the park at night. The reserve has tents and a camping place in the forest. The price is less than $5 for a tent (which can sleep two people). Bring insect repellant and other personal supplies. They have also recently constructed two cabins which can be rented for about $8.00 to $12.00 for 2 to 6 people. Contact the office for reservations.

Hours of Operation:

The park is open seven days per week, and staff is present at the reserve 24 hours a day, so visitors can arrive at any time. Entrance fee is C$90, or about $4.00. There is an additional charge if you wish to hire one of the guides to take you on the trails.

Contact Information:

Phone: 2278-3772
Website: www.chocoyero.com

Trails:

The reserve has several kilometers of hiking trails of different lengths and difficulty. The Chocoyero Trail follows the creek and leads to the waterfall where the parrots roost. It takes about 30 minutes from the entrance and is an easy walk. The trail to El Brujo is steep but not that long. The Congo Trail goes up into the hills and through a somewhat different forest type. There are several loop trails that take you through much of the reserve and a range of forest habitats.

The longest and most challenging trail leads up the mountain and takes six to seven hours to complete. It will take even longer if you stop frequently to bird, but you will have great views of the reserve and the surrounding area.

Description of Birding Sites:

Along the dirt road to the reserve, there are opportunities to observe birds in the forest and along the forest edge. This is a good place to watch for motmots, trogons and migrant warblers among other species as you approach the reserve.

The reserve trail system provides a chance to see any of the 183 species of birds that have been recorded here, including 44 neotropical migrants. They have also catalogued 56 kinds of mammals and 22 snakes, including two venomous species, although these are rarely seen from the trails. The main hiking trails lead through dry tropical forest habitat with semi-deciduous forest on the higher slopes.

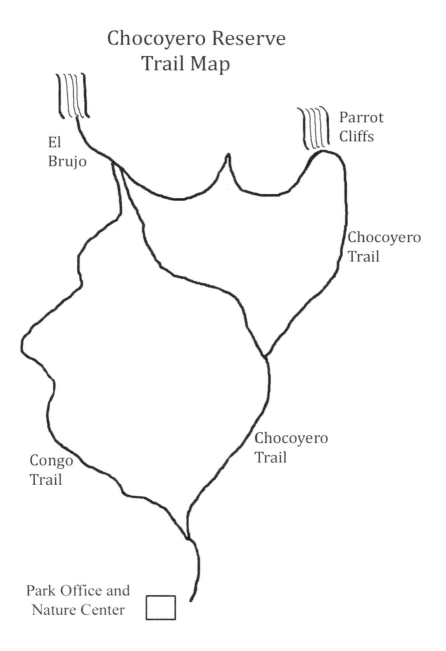

Chocoyero Reserve
Trail Map

El Brujo

Parrot Cliffs

Chocoyero Trail

Chocoyero Trail

Congo Trail

Park Office and Nature Center

Birds of Chocoyero El-Brujo Reserve

Plain Chachalaca
White-tailed Kite
Great Black-Hawk
Gray Hawk
Red-tailed Hawk
Red-billed Pigeon
Short-billed Pigeon
White-winged Dove
Common Ground-Dove
Plain-breasted Ground-Dove
Ruddy Ground-Dove
Inca Dove
White-tipped Dove
Squirrel Cuckoo
Groove-billed Ani
Barn Owl
Pacific Screech-Owl
Mottled Owl
Black-and-white Owl
Striped Owl
Common Paraque
Common Potoo
Vaux's Swift
Lesser Swallow-tailed Swift
Long-billed Hermit
Ruby-throated Hummingbird
Canivet's Emerald
Blue-tailed Hummingbird
Steely-vented Hummingbird
Cinnamon Hummingbird
Blue-throated Goldentail
Black-headed Trogon
Gartered Trogon
Elegant Trogon
Collared Trogon
Collared Aracari
Keel-billed Toucan
Hoffmann´s Woodpecker
Golden-olive Woodpecker
Pale-billed Woodpecker

Crested Caracara
Orange-fronted Parakeet
Barred Parakeet
Orange-chinned Parakeet
White-crowned Parrot
White-fronted Parrot
Barred Antshrike
Dusky Antbird
Plain-brown Woodcreeper
Streaked-headed Woodcreeper
Northern Beardless Tyrannulet
Greenish Elaenia
Ochre-bellied Flycatcher
Common Tody-Flycatcher
Yellow-olive Flycatcher
Eastern Wood-Pewee
Yellow-bellied Flycatcher
Acadian Flycatcher
Least Flycatcher
Yellowish Flycatcher
Dusky-capped Flycatcher
Great Crested Flycatcher
Brown-crested Flycatcher
Boat-billed Flycatcher
Sulphur-bellied Flycatcher
Eastern Kingbird
Scissor-tailed Flycatcher
Long-tailed Manakin
Black-crowned Tityra
Masked Tityra
Rose-throated Becard
Yellow-throated Vireo
Warbling Vireo
Red-eyed Vireo
Yellow-green Vireo
Lesser Greenlet
Rufous-browed Peppershrike
White-throated Magpie-Jay
Bank Swallow
Barn Swallow

Cliff Swallow
House Wren
Rufous-naped Wren
Banded Wren
Rufous-and-white Wren
Plain Wren
Swainson's Thrush
Wood Thrush
Clay-colored Thrush
Cedar Waxwing
Ovenbird
Louisiana Waterthrush
Northern Waterthrush
Blue-winged Warbler
Black-and-white Warbler
Tennessee Warbler
Gray-crowned Yellowthroat
Kentucky Warbler
Common Yellowthroat
Hooded Warbler
American Redstart
Tropical Parula
Magnolia Warbler
Yellow Warbler
Black-throated Green Warbler
Rufous-capped Warbler

Gray-headed Tanager
Blue-black Grassquit
Yellow-faced Grassquit
Grayish Saltator
Buff-throated Saltator
Black-headed Saltator
Olive Sparrow
Stripe-headed Sparrow
Hepatic Tanager
Summer Tanager
Western Tanager
Red-crowned Ant-Tanager
Red-throated Ant-Tanager
Rose-breasted Grosbeak
Blue Grosbeak
Indigo Bunting
Painted Bunting
Eastern Meadowlark
Melodious Blackbird
Bronzed Cowbird
Orchard Oriole
Baltimore Oriole
Yellow-billed Cacique
Montezuma Oropendola
Scrub Euphonia
Yellow-throated Euphonia

Specialties:

Thicket Tinamou
Crested Bobwhite
Double-toothed Kite
Laughing Falcon
Collared Forest-Falcon
Pacific Parakeet
Striped Cuckoo
Lesser Ground-Cuckoo

Blue-crowned Motmot
Turquoise-browed Motmot
Ruddy Woodcreeper
Ivory-billed Woodcreeper
Long-billed Gnatwren
Orange-billed Nightingale-Thrush
Worm-eating Warbler
Spot-breasted Oriole

Montibelli Reserve
(*La Reserva Silvestre Privada Montibelli*)

Site Description:

Montibelli Reserve, established in 2000, is a 165 hectare (400 acre) private reserve located on the range southwest of Managua, within the biological corridor between Chocoyero-El Brujo and Volcan Masaya National Park. It is located only 30 minutes from Managua. Due to its varying elevation of 360 to 770 meters (1,180 to 2,500 feet) above sea level, the area includes both tropical dry forest and semi-deciduous tropical forest. A total of 172 bird species have been recorded here. Several hectares are devoted to organic coffee and fruit production with the remainder as protected forest.

Directions:

From Managua, take the highway toward Masaya (Carretera Masaya). At the traffic circle at Km 14.4 turn right toward Ticuantepe, then take another right at the first traffic light (3.5 kilometers farther) in the direction of San Marcos (this road is called La Concha).

Go straight for a few kilometers past Juan Ramon Radilla Park and take a right at the first main road. Follow this for one block and then turn left. Follow the paved road and then turn right onto a dirt road where you see the Montibelli sign. It is about 2.5 km over this dirt road to the main lodge, known locally as La Casa Blanca. A high clearance vehicle is recommended, but the reserve can be accessed by car.

Public Transportation: By bus, find a microbus heading south to La Concha and get off at Km 18.5. From here you can take a taxi or hike to the reserve. This can be a dusty or muddy walk depending on the season. Arrangements for transportion can also be made with the office.

Access/accommodations:

The reserve has 4 two-person cabins and one lodge with four additional rooms. The cabins are constructed on the edge of a hillside overlooking the shade-grown coffee plantation and forest. Each cabin has a deck for easy birding. The lodge has two rooms on the lower level and two on the second floor. The rooms hold two to four people. All rooms come with private bathrooms and showers.

An outdoor dining area with kitchen and office are set away from guest lodging. The restaurant features family recipes and local dishes with Sunday barbecues. Cost per night is $75 per person, all meals included.

Among the staff is a naturalist and birder who can take you on the trails. Arrangements for guided hikes can be made with the office ahead of time when making reservations.

Contact Information:

Phone: Claudia Belli in Managua (2220-9801)
Email: info@montibelli.com
Website: www.montibelli.com

Trails:

Montibelli has 3 different trails with a total length of 6 km that also provide scenic overlooks with views of the Masaya Volcano and surrounding forest from the upper reaches. The trails vary between about one and three km in length and require from 30 minutes to 2½ hours to hike. If you are birding on these trails, it is possible to spend several hours to half a day on any of them.

Mirador Trail	750 meters	½ hour
Balcones Trail	2.5 km	2 hours
Pochote Trail	3 km	2 ½ hours

The trail system provides birding opportunities for one to two days. Chocoyero Reserve is located nearby for additional birding in the area, so this can serve as a base of operations for visiting other nearby sites. Bilingual guides are provided by the reserve and are usually required to hike the trails.

Description of Birding Sites:

Birding can be done along any of the trails that lead past coffee plantations and into the dry tropical forest. The trails follow the valleys formed between the hills and also extend higher up the hills. Recently, hummingbird feeders have been erected around the grounds that may attract several species. Birding can also be done from the deck by the cabins and lodge. During the rainy season the reserve is abundant with butterflies.

Montibelli Reserve

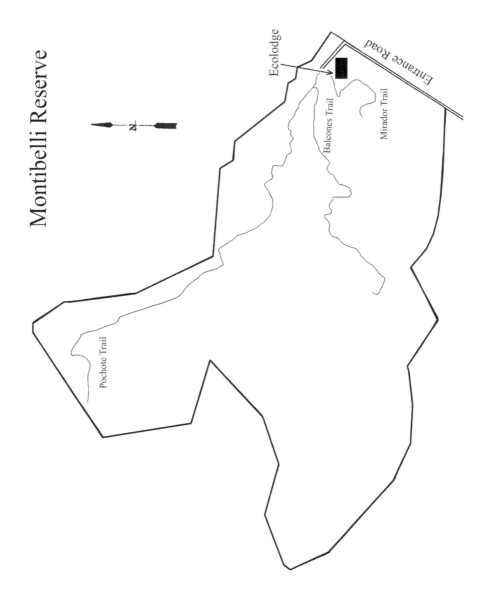

Ecolodge

Entrance Road

Balcones Trail

Mirador Trail

Pochote Trail

N

Birds of Montibelli Reserve

Plain Chachalaca	Streaked-headed Woodcreeper
White-tailed Hawk	Yellow-olive Flycatcher
Zone-tailed Hawk	**Acadian Flycatcher**
Short-tailed Hawk	Dusky-capped Flycatcher
Red-tailed Hawk	Nutting's Flycatcher
Roadside Hawk	Boat-billed Flycatcher
Gray Hawk	Sulphur-bellied Flycatcher
Broad-winged Hawk	Northern Beardless Tyrannulet
Great Black-Hawk	Western Kingbird
Red-billed Pigeon	Scissor-tailed Flycatcher
Ruddy Ground-Dove	Long-tailed Manakin
Inca Dove	Masked Tityra
Mottled Owl	Rose-throated Becard
Pacific Screech-Owl	Yellow-throated Vireo
Vaux's Swift	**Warbling Vireo**
White-necked Jacobin	Philadelphia Vireo
Little Hermit	Red-eyed Vireo
Stripe-throated Hermit	Lesser Greenlet
Blue-tailed Hummingbird	Rufous-browed Peppershrike
Cinnamon Hummingbird	White-throated Magpie-Jay
Rufous-tailed Hummingbird	Rufous-naped Wren
Green-breasted Mango	Banded Wren
Ruby-throated Hummingbird	Rufous-and-white Wren
Canivet's Emerald	Plain Wren
Black-headed Trogon	White-breasted Wood-Wren
Gartered Trogon	Swainson's Thrush
White-necked Puffbird	Wood Thrush
Collared Aracari	Clay-colored Thrush
Keel-billed Toucan	**Cedar Waxwing**
Hoffmann's Woodpecker	Ovenbird
Yellow-bellied Sapsucker	**Tennessee Warbler**
Peregrine Falcon	**Mourning Warbler**
Orange-fronted Parakeet	**Kentucky Warbler**
Orange-chinned Parakeet	Gray-crowned Yellowthroat
White-crowned Parrot	**Hooded Warbler**
White-fronted Parrot	**Tropical Parula**
Barred Antshrike	**Magnolia Warbler**
Dusky Antbird	**Chestnut-sided Warbler**
Slaty Antwen	Black-throated Green Warbler
Northern Barred Woodcreeper	Rufous-capped Warbler

Golden-crowned Warbler
Grayish Saltator
Buff-throated Saltator
Black-headed Saltator
Olive Sparrow
Black-striped Sparrow
Summer Tanager
Scarlet Tanager
Western Tanager
Red-throated Ant-Tanager
Red-crowned Ant-Tanager
Rose-breasted Grosbeak

Blue Grosbeak
Indigo Bunting
Painted Bunting
Melodious Blackbird
Orchard Oriole
Yellow-backed Oriole
Spot-breasted Oriole
Baltimore Oriole
Yellow-billed Cacique
Montezuma Oropendola
Scrub Euphonia
Yellow-throated Euphonia

Specialties:

Great Tinamou
Thicket Tinamou
Crested Bobwhite
Laughing Falcon
Collared Forest-Falcon
Pacific Parakeet
Turquoise-browed Motmot
Blue-crowned Motmot
Northern Potoo
Striped Cuckoo

Lesser Ground-Cuckoo
Steely-vented Hummingbird
Blue-throated Goldentail
Plain-capped Starthroat
Elegant Trogon
Long-billed Gnatwren
Orange-billed Nightingale-Thrush
Gray-headed Tanager
Yellow-green Vireo
Worm-eating Warbler

Black and White Owl

The Tisma Lagoon
(*Sistema Lagunar de Tisma*)

Site Description:

The Tisma Lagoon and wetland complex is located to the east of Managua in the lowlands created between Nicaragua's two largest lakes—Lake Nicaragua and Lake Managua. The lagoon extends off of the Tipitapa River and is surrounded by a vast wetland. Tisma is a fairly unexplored lake and wetland area and provides habitat for a variety of aquatic and terrestrial animals. The Tisma Lagoon is part of a larger protected wetland area that encompasses 16,850 hectares (41,600 acres).

Tisma Lagoon was established as a natural reserve in 1983. It is one of Nicaragua's Important Bird Area (IBA) and was recognized as a Wetland of International Importance (Ramsar Site) in 2001. The lake is about 10 square kilometers in size with a depth of one to six meters (3 to 20 feet).

The lagoon is an important site for waterfowl and other marsh birds. Tremendous flocks of birds and a variety of other animals can be found in the wetlands, including a number of wintering North American species.

Directions:

From Managua, continue east on the main road (PanAm Highway), which goes past the international airport toward Tipitapa. As you approach Tititapa, turn right onto Hwy 11. Turn south towards Masaya and continue to Km 46, then turn left towards the town of Tisma. Follow this road 13 km to Tisma.

Once in Tisma, there should be a sign directing you to the lagoon or just ask for the "road to the beach". It is another 3.5 km and a four-wheel drive vehicle is required to get there, particularly in the wet season. In Tisma, arrangements can be made with the local tourist office or fisherman to get a boat to explore the lagoon and surrounding wetlands.

Public Transportation: Buses leave Managua to Masaya or Tipitapa. From there take a bus to Tisma. It will require at least 45 minutes to reach the town of Tisma. Cost of the bus is about $1.50.

Access/Accommodations:

Food and limited services are available in the town of Tisma. The lagoon and wetland complex is a day-use area only. This site is relatively easy to visit from Managua, Granada, or Masaya. Boat tours of the area are available for about $15 to $20 per person, depending on the size of the group.

Tisma Lagoon and Wetlands

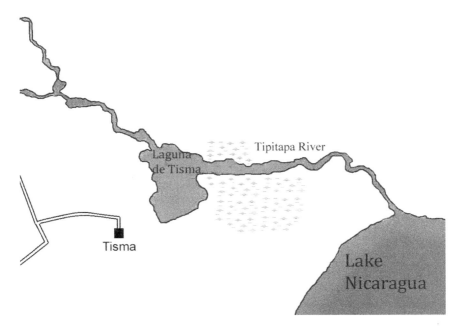

Description of Birding Sites:

Tisma Lagoon and the surrounding wetlands provide important habitat for a wide range of birds. However, water levels vary in this wetland complex and during periods of low water the vast flocks that this site is known for disperse to other areas.

This site has long been one of the best places to observe the Nicaraguan Grackle, among other species. The following list was compiled during surveys for Ramsar designation and is a preliminary list of recorded species. This site is likely to contain a number of rails and many other wetland species that have not been adequately surveyed here.

Birds of Tisma

Thicket Tinamou
Black-bellied Whistling-Duck
Muscovy Duck
Blue-winged Teal
Northern Shoveler
Lesser Scaup
Plain Chachalaca
Crested Bobwhite
Neotropic Cormorant
Anhinga
Great Blue Heron
Great Egret
Little Blue Heron
Tricolored Heron
Cattle Egret
Green Heron
Black-crowned Night-Heron
White Ibis
Sora
Purple Gallinule
American Coot
Northern Jacana
Spotted Sandpiper

Solitary Sandpiper
Whimbrel
Long-billed Dowitcher
Laughing Gull
Herring Gull
Gull-billed Tern
Short-billed Pigeon
White-winged Dove
Mourning Dove
Inca Dove
Groove-billed Ani
Barred Forest-Falcon
Collared Forest-Falcon
Crested Caracara
Turquoise-browed Motmot
Scissor-tailed Flycatcher
White-throated Magpie-Jay
Barn Swallow
Rufous-naped Wren
Red-winged Blackbird
Melodious Blackbird
Altamira Oriole
Montezuma Oropendola

Specialties

Jabiru	Limpkin
Wood Stork	American Golden Plover
Gray-headed Kite	Wilson's Plover
Short-tailed Hawk	Black-necked Stilt
Nicaraguan Grackle	

Gray-necked Wood-Rail

Additional Sites

Chiltepe Peninsula Natural Reserve
(*Reserva Natural Peninsula de Chiltepe*)

Chiltepe Peninsula Natural Reserve is located on the south shore of Lake Managua. It is 15 km northwest of Managua and being close to the city is a popular destination for local visitors. The forested areas and adjacent lake shore provide habitat for a wide range of bird species. This is a day-use area only and also a possible site for observing the Nicaraguan Grackle

Among the threats affecting this protected area are frequent forest fires and agricultural encroachment into the nature reserve.

Monte Galan Lagoon
(*Laguna de Monte Galán*)

The Monte Galan Lagoon formed at the foot of the Momotombo Volcano in a narrow valley. The lagoon is located on the west side of the volcano and is surrounded by a forest remnant. Several hot springs are found around the lake.

Monte Galan is located near the town of Momotombo and the ruins of León Viejo, a UNESCO World Heritage Site. To reach this site you will need to hike a trail of loose stone along the foot of Momotombo. For those hiking onto the slopes of Momotombo, the lake can be seen from the west side of this immense volcano. This site is a day-use area only and relatively near to Managua.

Quelantaro Wildlife Reserve
(*Reserve Silvestre Privada Quelantaro*)

Site Description:

Quelantaro is a privately-owned nature reserve located about 45 minutes southwest of Managua in the municipality of Villa El Carmen. It is 70 acres in size, of which 80% is a designated conservation area of dry forest. This reserve is one of Nicaragua's seven active MoSI stations, a bird banding site for monitoring resident and migrant bird populations.

Quelantaro was designated as a private wildlife reserve in 2003 and acquired by the current owners in 2006. In addition to the bird conservation efforts, this reserve also has a sea turtle monitoring program and is focusing on ecotourism in the communities of Villa El Carmen.

Location: Quelantaro is located west of Managua in the municipality of Villa El Carmen, in the Department of Managua, at Km 46 on the side road. Taking the main highway from Managua to Masaya, travel to Km 10.5. This is the turn off to the reserve.

Contact:

Phone:	El Carmen office - 2265-4811
	Managua office - 8633-7958
Email:	quelantaroni@gmail.com or ocamgua@yahoo.es
	galinicaragua@yahoo.es
Website:	quelantaronica.bligoo.com/ (in Spanish),
	Villa El Carmen: www.reservasilvestres.com.

The Cardones Eco Lodge in Villa El Carmen:

Phone:	Managua 8364-5925
Email:	loscardonesecolodge@gmail.com.
Website:	www.loscardones.com

The Pacific Lowlands

Gartered Trogon

Region 1
The Pacific Lowlands;
The Land of Lakes and Volcanoes

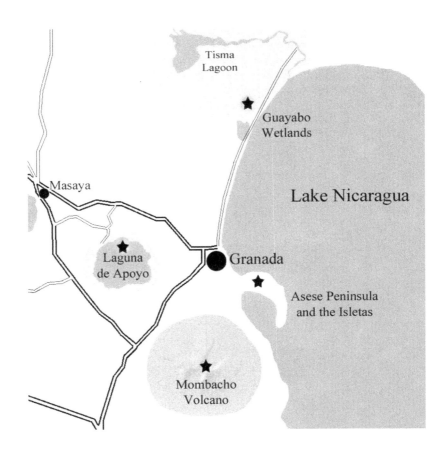

The Granada area lies where the dry tropical forest and farmland meet the shores of Lake Nicaragua. This vast inland sea and the surrounding area has four featured sites with diverse habitats that can easily be reached from Granada, providing several days of birding opportunities.

Birding Sites in the Granada Area

Granada is located 47 km from Managua and can be reached in about one hour from the capital by car or express bus. Granada was founded in 1524 and is the oldest city established on the mainland of the Americas. The city has been the capital several times before Managua was chosen and nowadays, Granada is the city most visited by tourists in Nicaragua.

Granada is located on the northwest shore of Lake Nicaragua, an enormous freshwater lake that contains two large volcanic islands and hundreds of small islands, known as the Isletas. The city is well defined by its many colonial buildings and you can easily reach Lake Nicaragua by walking down La Calzada Street. There is a park located along the lakeshore that provides some good birding opportunities, or continue on to Asese Bay to explore the lake by boat or kayak.

A dirt road going north from the city follows the lakeshore, which provides some additional birding opportunities and is a good place to watch for Nicaraguan grackle. This road can be taken for about 22 km along the shore of the lake and past some small lakes and wetlands.

Day trips can be made from here to the Mombacho Volcano, Laguna de Apoyo, the isletas, and numerous other sites. Additional sites in the Granada area include La Calera Private Reserve and a new private reserve is being developed on the south side of Mombacho, called Mecetepe, which contains dry forest, wetlands, and lagoons.

Some of the sites nearby Managua, such as Chocoyero-El Brujo and Montibelli, can easily be reached from Granada. Many foreigners rent or own property in this city, and the large number of tourists that visit here has encouraged a wide range of facilities to be available and easily found here. This makes Granada not only a pleasant city to visit but a good base to undertake day trips to a variety of birding sites. In winter months, large flocks of Scissor-tailed Flycatchers gather over the city at sunset as they head to their evening roost.

Lake Apoyo
(*Laguna de Apoyo*)

Site Description:

Nicaragua's most scenic lake is Laguna de Apoyo, just outside of Masaya. This lake formed as the crater of the long extinct Apoyo Volcano collapsed. The lake is at least 800 feet deep—the lowest point in all of Central America. Considering how easy it is to reach the lake, tourist development is rather limited. Despite its continued seismic activity, the volcano is generally considered dormant, and a dense forest has grown up the slopes. An earthquake in 2000 under the crater-rim town of Caterina caused Apoyo's water to slosh back and forth and damaged several homes. The crater slopes contain a few hiking trails, but the area has been protected from further development. The crater lake also hosts a few endemic fish species found nowhere else on earth.

A great scenic overlook of Lake Apoyo is located at the village of Caterina. This is located uphill from the city square. There is another vantage point in Diriá at the El Boquete overlook from where you can enjoy a great view of the Lake Apoyo.

Directions:

Several roads lead to the junction with the main road to the bottom of the crater. The easiest way to get there is to take the highway from Masaya to Granada. At Km 37.4, turn by the communication tower onto a cobblestone road. Follow this for 3 km, then turn left at the T-intersection. Go 1.2 km and then turn right at another T-intersection. After only 0.2 km turn left to the entrance road to the reserve. From here it is another 2.5 km down a steep road to the bottom of the crater.

There is another very scenic road that approaches the reserve from the town of Caterina. To reach this, take the highway from Managua to Masaya and turn at the round-about to Caterina. In Caterina, go to the city square and then follow the road along the rim of the crater for several kilometers to where it intersects with the reserve entrance.

The cobblestone road winds through rural residential neighborhoods and small farms to the edge of the crater reserve. From here, a road descends steeply down into the crater. Once at the bottom, you can slowly drive the paved and dirt roads going either direction parallel to the lakeshore.

At the bottom the road forks to follow the lakeshore. Turning right will lead to the Narome Lodge. Follow this road past the lodge for about 1.5 km where it ends at a large private residence. Going in the other direction from the intersection you can follow this road for several kilometers as it winds past an area of largely residential land and some resorts along the shore of the lake. After the first two kilometers it is mostly small farms with better habitat. A morning walk on this road can produce a nice variety of forest and forest edge species.

Access/accommodations:

There are a number of places to eat or lodge along the western shore of the crater lake. At any establishment, pay $6 to $10 to stay for the day with extra charges for lodging and food.

Guided hikes can be arranged with the Lake Apoyo Biological Station (Estación Biológica Laguna de Apoyo), located along the lower crater road. They offer a one-hour birding excursion for $5 and three-hour tour of the area for $15.

Information is available at: http://www.gaianicaragua.org.

Contact Information:

The Biological Station and several of the lodges along the lakeshore can provide information as well as most hotels in the cities of Masaya and Granada. Most offer scenic tours rather than birding tours.

Trails:

There is a hiking trail that leads to the top of the crater. Inquire with local businesses at the bottom for directions. Otherwise, walk or drive the road descending the crater and those at the bottom of the crater.

Description of Birding Sites:

In Lake Apoyo Nature Reserve, 225 bird species have been documented. Several birds are associated with the waters of Lake Apoyo, others with the forest habitats. Lake Apoyo Nature Reserve has lots of easily accessible, tropical dry forest habitat and shore areas for birdwatching.

The most accessible birding around Lake Apoyo is to follow the area roads, particularly the steep road that descends the crater to the shores of the lake and the road at the bottom of the crater. Drive slowly and stop for any birds seen or heard. Usually the traffic is very light and you should be able to stop almost anywhere where you can leave enough room for another vehicle to get by.

Once you reach the bottom of the crater there is a road that parallels the lake shore for some distance, leading to a few resorts, private homes, and small farms. The best birding is by taking the road to the left, which leads through dry tropical forest and forest edge habitat. Travel to the end of the cobblestone road (about 1.5 km) and walk the dirt road beyond this for another 2 km. This is also one of the best places to find Canivet's Emerald. Watch around flowering shrubs planted by entrances to some of the homes.

The lake also attracts a variety of waterbirds, including grebes, ducks, Osprey and a variety of herons and egrets. You will need to enter one of the resorts to get a good look at the lake.

From the lake shore, watch overhead for soaring vultures and hawks. Another option is to watch these soaring birds from the rim of the crater from the village of Caterina or other vantage points along the upper road.

Hoffmann's Woodpecker

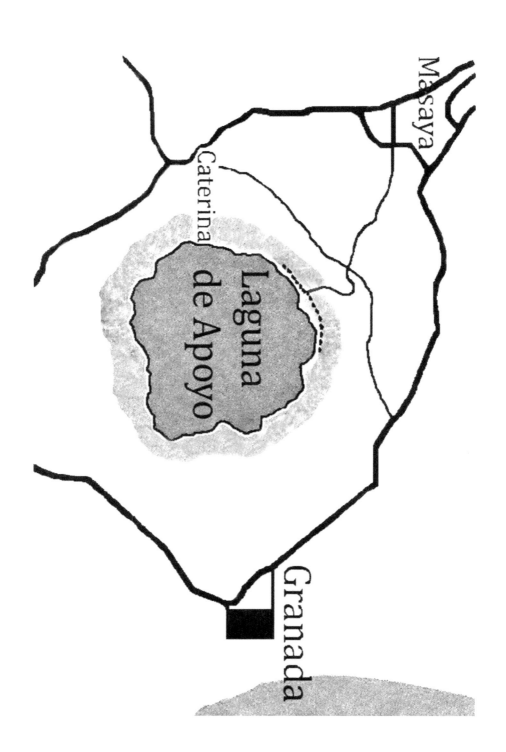

Birds of Lake Apoyo

Black-bellied Whistling-Duck
Blue-winged Teal
Pied-billed Grebe
Wood Stork
Magnificent Frigatebird
Brown Pelican
Bare-throated Tiger-Heron
Great Blue Heron
Great Egret
Snowy Egret
Little Blue Heron
Tricolored Heron
Cattle Egret
Green Heron
Black-crowned Night-Heron
Yellow-crowned Night-Heron
Osprey
White-tailed Kite
Great Black-Hawk
Roadside Hawk
Broad-winged Hawk
Gray Hawk
Short-tailed Hawk
White-tailed Hawk
Swainson's Hawk
Zone-tailed Hawk
Northern Jacana
Spotted Sandpiper
Laughing Gull
Ring-billed Gull
Black Tern
Red-billed Pigeon
White-winged Dove
Mourning Dove
Inca Dove
Common Ground-Dove
Ruddy Ground-Dove
White-tipped Dove
Squirrel Cuckoo
Yellow-billed Cuckoo

Groove-billed Ani
Barn Owl
Pacific Screech-Owl
Spectacled Owl
Ferruginous Pygmy-Owl
Mottled Owl
Striped Owl
Lesser Nighthawk
Common Nighthawk
Common Paraque
Chuck-will's-widow
Common Potoo
Chimney Swift
Vaux's Swift
Little Hermit
Green-breasted Mango
Plain-capped Starthroat
Ruby-thr. Hummingbird
Blue-chested Hummingbird
Blue-tailed Hummingbird
Steely-vented Hummingbird
Rufous-tailed Hummingbird
Cinnamon Hummingbird
Black-headed Trogon
Gartered Trogon
Elegant Trogon
Blue-crowned Motmot
Turquoise-browed Motmot
Ringed Kingfisher
Belted Kingfisher
Collared Aracari
Keel-billed Toucan
Hoffmann's Woodpecker
Pale-billed Woodpecker
Crested Caracara
Laughing Falcon
American Kestrel
Merlin
Peregrine Falcon
Green Parakeet

Orange-fronted Parakeet
Orange-chinned Parakeet
White-crowned Parrot
White-fronted Parrot
Yellow-naped Parrot
Barred Antshrike
Streak-chested Antpitta
Olivaceous Woodcreeper
Plain-brown Woodcreeper
Ruddy Woodcreeper
No. Barred Woodcreeper
Streaked-headed Woodcreeper
Spot-crowned Woodcreeper
Northern Beardless Tyrannulet
Yellow Tyrannulet
Greenish Elaenia
Paltry Tyrannulet
Yellow-olive Flycatcher
Olive-sided Flycatcher
Eastern Wood-Pewee
Tropical Pewee
Yellow-bellied Flycatcher
Least Flycatcher
Dusky-capped Flycatcher
Ash-throated Flycatcher
Nutting's Flycatcher
Great Crested Flycatcher
Brown-crested Flycatcher
Boat-billed Flycatcher
Sulphur-bellied Flycatcher
Western Kingbird
Eastern Kingbird
Scissor-tailed Flycatcher
Long-tailed Manakin
Masked Tityra
Rose-throated Becard
Yellow-throated Vireo
Blue-headed Vireo
Warbling Vireo
Philadelphia Vireo
Red-eyed Vireo
Yellow-green Vireo

Lesser Greenlet
No. Rough-wing. Swallow
Purple Martin
Gray-breasted Martin
Tree Swallow
Bank Swallow
Barn Swallow
Cliff Swallow
Rufous-naped Wren
Banded Wren
Rufous-and-white Wren
Plain Wren
White-lored Gnatcatcher
Veery
Swainson's Thrush
Wood Thrush
Clay-colored Thrush
Black-and-white Warbler
Prothonotary Warbler
Tennessee Warbler
Mourning Warbler
Common Yellowthroat
American Redstart
Cerulean Warbler
Magnolia Warbler
Blackburnian Warbler
Yellow Warbler
Chestnut-sided Warbler
Townsend's Warbler
Black-thr. Blue Warbler
Black-thr. Green Warbler
Rufous-capped Warbler
Blue-gray Tanager
Blue-black Grassquit
Olive Sparrow
Stripe-headed Sparrow
Summer Tanager
Scarlet Tanager
Western Tanager
Rose-breasted Grosbeak
Blue-black Grosbeak
Blue Grosbeak

Indigo Bunting
Painted Bunting
Melodious Blackbird
Bronzed Cowbird
Giant Cowbird

Orchard Oriole
Altamira Oriole
Baltimore Oriole
Montezuma Oropendola
Scrub Euphonia

Specialties:

Thicket Tinamou
Plain Chachalaca
Crested Bobwhite
Least Grebe
Lesser Yellow-headed Vulture
Mississippi Kite
Double-striped Thick-Knee
Mangrove Cuckoo
Striped Cuckoo
Pheasant Cuckoo

Lesser Ground-Cuckoo
Canivet's Emerald
Blue-throated Goldentail
White-necked Puffbird
Pied Puffbird
Barred Forest-Falcon
Collared Forest-Falcon
Bat Falcon
Yellow-bellied Flycatcher
White-throated Magpie-Jay
Gray-headed Tanager

White-throated Magpie-Jay

Mombacho Volcano
(*Volcan Mombacho*)

Site Description:

The Mombacho Volcano is one of the more prominent volcanoes in Nicaragua and after the Masaya Volcano is also one of the most accessible. The reserve was established in 1983, but it took another five years (1985 to 1990) to construct the road to the summit where an array of communications towers was built. The biological station was built in 1996 and a major trail building project was undertaken in 2001.

The entrance to the reserve is located only 10 km from Granada. There is a very steep road (in the native Nahuatl language, Mombacho means steep) that leads to the top of this dormant volcano. There you will find a rustic visitor center where you can obtain guides and information about the reserve. The reserve encompasses 578 hectares (1,425 acres) of core protected area and another 6,644 hectares (16,417 acres) of buffer zone.

Varied habitats include a dry tropical forest at the bottom of the volcano, coffee plantations further up the slope and cloud forest at the summit. A total of 227 species of birds have been recorded here.

It will take about 20-30 minutes to reach the top of the volcano by transport. The Mombacho Reserve is run by the Cocibolca Foundation and offers more services to tourists than many other local attractions. The visitor center has trail maps, information about the flora and fauna, a topographic model of the volcano, guides for hire, and a few souvenirs. There is also a cafeteria that provides small meals and drinks.

Because of its height of 1,345 meters (4,045 feet), a cloud forest and elfin forest exist on the upper reaches of the volcano. These particular habitats have a high species richness and contain many unique plants, including numerous orchids. Also, because this forest is isolated from other similar vegetation, forming an island of habitat, several endemic plant and animal species have evolved among the forests of Mombacho Volcano. When you arrive at the summit the temperature will be much cooler with high humidity. It is almost always windy here, so bring a windbreaker and umbrella or raincoat for mist and showers that occur, especially in the afternoon.

The Mombacho Volcano has four craters, all of which are covered in dense cloud forest. This type of forest is only found at one other spot on the Pacific side of Nicaragua, on the Maderas Volcano on Ometepe Island. On Mombacho there is a short trail around one of the craters and longer trails to several other craters.

In addition to the different trees and plants that thrive here you may also observe howler and white face monkeys, amphibians, and reptiles. The Mombacho salamander is the most noteworthy endemic species. This small salamander is only found on the upper reaches of Mombacho.

The bird life in this cloud forest can be difficult to observe and is not extremely diverse, but a number of interesting species can be found here. The variety of birds in the cloud forest is quite different from those found in the lower forests and shade grown coffee plantations, which tend to harbor a greater diversity of birds.

Directions:

Take Highway 6 southwest out of Granada. The entrance to the reserve is located at a junction called El Guanacaste, at Km 50 on the highway between Granada and Nandaime. Turn left onto a cobblestone road at the El Guanacaste intersection, which is marked by a sign to the reserve. The main highway becomes the Pan-American Highway to Nandaime, while a right turn leads to Diria, Diriomo, and Caterina.

Traveling from Managua, take the highway through Masaya and then turn right toward Catarina at the first round-about after Masaya. Continue until the road ends at the El Guanacaste intersection. You will see the Mombacho Volcano directly ahead of you.

About 2 km up a cobblestone road is the park entrance that is situated on the foot of the volcano. A parking lot is located here. You can bird the lower trails or take the transport truck to the top. The truck ascends the volcano four times a day.

The ride uphill is quite an adventure in itself. The steepness of the road is an experience as you ascend nearly 4,000 feet, traveling through coffee plantations in the lower elevations that give way to cloud forest.

Public Transportation: You can take a bus from Granada or Nandaime, or even from Managua to reach the reserve entrance. Taxis will also find the road to the reserve entrance, saving the hike from the highway.

Access/accommodations:

The visitor center provides information and maps to the hiking trails. There is also lodging available at the summit. Cost is around $45 per person and includes dinner and breakfast. Contact Granada M.I.A about the Eco Albergue Mombacho Lodge can be found in area hotels.

Hours of operation:

The reserve is open to the public from Friday through Sunday, from 8:00 am to 5:00 pm. The truck uphill leaves at 8:30 am, 10:00 am, 1:00 pm and 3:00 pm. For early morning birding, consider staying overnight in the bunk house located on the upper level of the visitor center at the summit of Mombacho.

The entrance fee plus transportation in the truck costs about $8.00 (C$150). It is no longer possible to take a private vehicle to the summit, due to driving hazards on the steep road and one-way traffic.

The reserve is closed on Monday. On Tuesday and Wednesday the reserve is closed unless there are enough reservations. The reserve will open if there are at least ten people. So if you have a group of ten people just call and let them know. If you have less than ten, call to see if there are other people wanting to visit that day.

Contact Information:

Phone: 2552-5858
Website: www.mombacho.org (in Spanish)
       www.mombotour.com (in English)
Ecolodge: 8988-1199 or granadamia.ni@gmail.com

Trails: There are three different trails available to explore the area, with hikes varying in duration between 30 minutes to four hours. In addition to observing the diverse flora and fauna, you can also enjoy some superb views of the area around the volcano when clear skies permit.

Tigrillo Trail

Duration: 2 1/2 hours—800 m

A coffee plantation trail located outside of the reserve at Hacienda El Progreso. Information at http://cafelasflores.com/coffee-ecoadventure.

El Crater Trail

Duration: 1 hour and 30 minutes—2 km
Difficulty: Medium
Dense cloud forest and views of Lake Nicaragua, weather permitting.

El Puma Trail

Duration: 4 hours—4 km. Difficulty: Challenging but spectacular hike.

On the Puma Trail you see different types of forest and wonderful views of the surrounding landscape. Several platforms provide superb views and expose visitors to the strong wind on the volcano.

You cannot enter the Puma Trail without a guide, but you can do the crater trail on your own. The Crater Trail is well developed with interpretive signs (in Spanish) that focus on the plants and forest. Guides for the Puma Trail cost $10 for a group of up to ten people and $5.00 for the Crater Trail.

For the ambitious visitor, you can hike the road to the top of the volcano, but be advised that this is a very steep road. Walking down this road is actually more difficult than going up.

Description of Birding Sites:

On the lower and mid-slopes the volcano is covered in dry tropical forest, with open fields and shade-grown coffee plantations. The upper reaches of the volcano are covered in cloud forest with elfin forest on the exposed slopes. Both areas have been developed with good hiking trails, and the birds are as different as the habitat between the lower slopes and the summit.

Rufous-capped Warbler

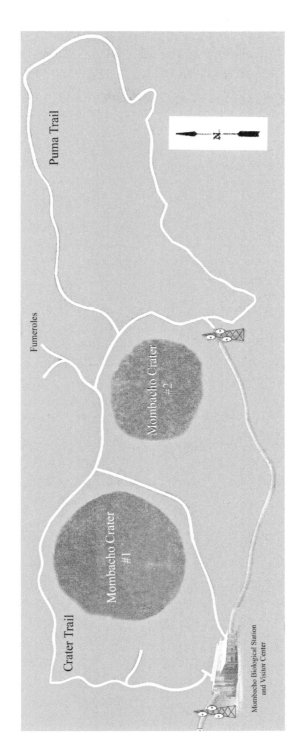

69

Birds of Mombacho

Plain Chachalaca
Crested Bobwhite
White-tailed Kite
Swallow-tailed Kite
Plumbeous Kite
Cooper's Hawk
Bicolored Hawk
White-tailed Hawk
White Hawk
Gray Hawk
Short-tailed Kite
Red-tailed Hawk
Blue Ground-Dove
Gray-headed Dove
Pacific Screech-Owl
Spectacled Owl
Ferruginous Pygmy-Owl
Mottled Owl
Black-and-white Owl
Stripe-throated Hermit
Canivet's Emerald
Blue-throated Hummingbird
Blue-tailed Hummingbird
Steely-vented Hummingbird
Cinnamon Hummingbird
Black-headed Trogon
Gartered Trogon
Blue-crowned Motmot
Turquoise-browed Motmot
White-necked Puffbird
Collared Aracari
Keel-billed Toucan
Hoffmann's Woodpecker
Smoky-brown Woodpecker
Golden-olive Woodpecker
Pale-billed Woodpecker
Crested Caracara
Laughing Falcon
American Kestrel
Peregrine Falcon

Crimson-fronted Parakeet
Orange-fronted Parakeet
Orange-chinned Parakeet
White-fronted Parrot
Red-lored Parrot
Yellow-naped Parrot
Barred Antshrike
Dusky Antbird
Olivaceous Woodcreeper
Plain-brown Woodcreeper
Northern Barred Woodcreeper
Streaked-headed Woodcreeper
Spot-crowned Woodcreeper
Plain Xenops
Greenish Elaenia
Ochre-bellied Flycatcher
Northern Bentbill
Common Tody-Flycatcher
Yellow-olive Flycatcher
Yellow-margined Flycatcher
Olive-sided Flycatcher
Western Wood-Pewee
Eastern Wood-Pewee
Tropical Pewee
Yellow-bellied Flycatcher
Acadian Flycatcher
White-throated Flycatcher
Least Flycatcher
Yellowish Flycatcher
Dusky-capped Flycatcher
Great Crested Flycatcher
Brown-crested Flycatcher
Sulphur-bellied Flycatcher
Western Kingbird
Long-tailed Manakin
Masked Tityra
Yellow-throated Vireo
Blue-headed Vireo
Warbling Vireo
Philadelphia Vireo

Red-eyed Vireo
Yellow-green Vireo
Lesser Greenlet
White-throated Magpie-Jay
Bank Swallow
Cliff Swallow
Rufous-naped Wren
Banded Wren
Plain Wren
Long-billed Gnatwren
Blue-gray Gnatcatcher
Tropical Gnatcatcher
Swainson's Thrush
Wood Thrush
Cedar Waxwing
Ovenbird
Worm-eating Warbler
Louisiana Waterthrush
Northern Waterthrush
Golden-winged Warbler
Black-and-white Warbler
Prothonotary Warbler
Tennessee Warbler
Gray-crowned Yellowthroat
Mourning Warbler
Kentucky Warbler
Hooded Warbler
American Redstart
Cerulean Warbler
Tropical Parula
Magnolia Warbler
Blackburnian Warbler

Yellow Warbler
Chestnut-sided Warbler
Black-throated Blue Warbler
Yellow-rumped Warbler
Townsend's Warbler
Black-throated Green Warbler
Rufous-capped Warbler
Canada Warbler
Wilson's Warbler
Gray-headed Tanager
Red-legged Honeycreeper
Black-headed Saltator
Black-striped Sparrow
Stripe-headed Sparrow
Olive Sparrow
Summer Tanager
Scarlet Tanager
Western Tanager
White-winged Tanager
Red-crowned Ant-Tanager
Red-throated Ant-Tanager
Rose-breasted Grosbeak
Blue Grosbeak
Indigo Bunting
Painted Bunting
Dickcissel
Streak-backed Oriole
Baltimore Oriole
Montezuma Oropendola
Scrub Euphonia
Yellow-crowned Euphonia
Olive-backed Euphonia

Specialties of the Cloud Forest:

Purple-throated Mountain-gem
Magnificent Hummingbird
Plain-capped Starthroat

Steely-vented Hummingbird
Mountain Elaenia
Chestnut-capped Brush-Finch

Specialties of the mid and lower slopes:

Thicket Tinamou
Crested Guan
Great Currasow
King Vulture
Collared Forest-Falcon
Red-billed Pigeon
Green Parakeet
Lesser Ground-Cuckoo
Little Hermit
Long-billed Starthroat

Pied Puffbird
Ruddy Woodcreeper
Ivory-billed Woodcreeper
Northern Beardless Tyrannulet
Stub-tailed Spadebill
Eye-ringed Flatbill
White-ruffed Manakin
Rufous-and-white Wren
Cinnamon-bellied Flowerpiercer
Red-legged Honeycreeper

Montezuma Oropendula

Lake Road and Guayabo Wetlands
(*Humedales de Guayabo*)

Site Description:

Lake Nicaragua, also called Lago Cocibolca, is the tenth largest freshwater lake in the world, and the second largest in Latin America after Lake Titicaca in South America. Cocibolca means "sweet sea" in the native language. It is approximately 100 miles long and 20 miles wide and is connected to the Caribbean Sea through the San Juan River. It was of great strategic value as it enabled European explorers and settlers to access Nicaragua's interior once they entered this vast lake. The site for the city of Granada was chosen due to its tactical advantages.

Lake Nicaragua provides habitat for a variety of gulls, terns, waders and shorebirds. A variety of herons and egrets as well as Limpkin and Northern Jacana can be found in the shallows and even Magnificent Frigatebirds may visit as they drift inland from the nearby Pacific Ocean.

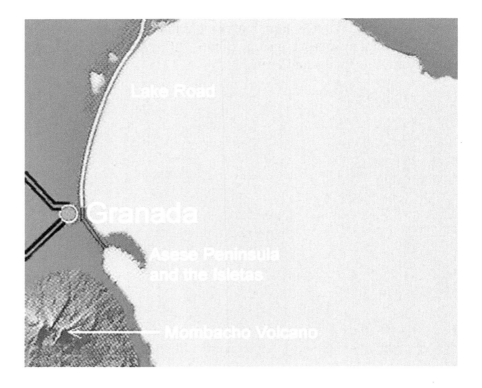

Description of Birding Sites:

Two roads follow the lake shore from the City of Granada. One stretch goes south through the city park and along the shore and eventually leads to the Asese Peninsula. The woodlots alongside the road and the shore can be rewarding. To reach the park, go east along La Calzada Street from the central plaza. At the end, turn right to drive through the park and along the lake shore. A small fee is charged at the park entrance. This road continues south to Asese Bay and Peninsula with access to the isletas. It is not recommended to walk in the park after dark.

There also is a road that goes north of town along the lakeshore for more than 20 km. This is known as the Malacatoya Road, leading along the lake to the El Guayabo Wetlands. To find this road, take Santa Lucia Street to its end at the Lake Granada shoreline and head north (left) in the direction of Malacotoya. This road goes along the lake and among small farms and houses, but intermittent wetlands and scrub provide fair to good habitat. It can be difficult to see the lakeshore in many areas, but some of the shallows attract herons, ergets, shorebirds, gulls, and terns.

Birds of the Area

Lake Nicaragua and its adjacent wetlands provide important habitat for migrant waterfowl and shorebirds as well as nesting waders and other species. During migration, swallows will take advantage of the abundant swarms of non-biting flies that hatch from the lake. Flocks of literally hundreds can be seen, comprised of numerous species. This area was also at one time among the best places to observe Nicaraguan grackle, Nicaragua's best known near-endemic.

Common Birds of Guayabo Wetlands

Fulvous Whistling-Duck	Caspian Tern
Great Egret	Laughing Gull
Little Blue Heron	Gray-breasted Martin
Tricolored Heron	Mangrove Swallow
Rufescent Tiger-Heron	No. Rough-winged Swallow
Northern Jacana	Cliff Swallow
Black-necked Stilt	Barn Swallow
Purple Gallinule	Tropical Mockingbird

Specialties:

Pearl Kite	Long-billed Dowitcher
Snail Kite	Black Skimmer
Peregrine Falcon	

The Little Islands of Granada
(*Las Isletas de Granada*)

Site Description:

The Little Islands, locally called Las Isletas, are comprised of an archipelago of 365 islands of volcanic origin along the northwest coast of Lake Nicaragua, just off of Granada. Many of these islands have been developed by wealthy businessmen and foreigners as elaborate second homes. However, the shoreline and backwaters around these islands harbor a variety of wetland birds. Tours can be arranged through most of the hotels in Granada. The standard tours last about an hour and tend to focus on the homes of the rich and famous. However, nature tours and special arrangements can be made with any of the tour operators. Most of the boat operators know some of the birds and will give you their Spanish names but are not birders themselves.

You can also enjoy the bird life around the islands by renting a kayak or small boat with electric motor. It is also possible to access some of the islands, as several of them feature restaurants or lodging.

Directions: Tours can be arranged in Granada, however the boat tours from Asese provide access to much better bird habitat on the south side of the peninsula than the north side.

From Granada, drive east along La Calzada Street from the central plaza. At the lake, turn right to drive along the lake shore and through the park. Continue to the end to where the road turns toward Asese Bay. Here is a marina where you can hire a boat and operator or make arrangements to tour the area by kayak.

Access and accommodations:

Access to the park is by foot or car, while a trip around the isletas will require a boat. This is a day-use area with abundant places to stay in Granada. Tours and boat rental information can be obtained at most hotels and any tour company in the city.

Contact:

Check with the information desk at any hotel in Granada for tour information and reservations.

Description of Birding Sites:

Birding is along the shore of Lake Nicaragua in the city park and upland woods along the area roads leading toward the peninsula. The best aquatic habitat is on the Asese Bay side of the peninsula among the backwaters and open water around the isletas. Along the shore of Asese Bay and around any of the undeveloped islands there is abundant forested and wetland habitat with a variety of herons, egrets, and other waders and aquatic birds, plus a range of passerines among the woodlands.

You can take a boat tour or rent a small boat to wander throughout the area exploring the many hidden corners among the islands to search for a variety of birds. Rentals are available for small boats with electric motors for one to three people.

If you are taking a watercraft by yourself, be sure to get a map. The many bays and inlets among the islands can be challenging to navigate. Also, beware of rough water when winds are from the south

Birds of the Isletas

Blue-winged Teal
Pied-billed Grebe
Least Grebe
Neotropic Cormorant
Anhinga
Great Blue Heron
Great Egret
Tricolored Heron
Little Blue Heron
Black-crowned Night-Heron
Common Gallinule
Purple Gallinule
Northern Jacana
Laughing Gull

Caspian Tern
Short-billed Pigeon
Common Ground-Dove
Inca Dove
Orange-fronted Parakeet
White-fronted Parrot
Osprey
Ringed Kingfisher
Belted Kingfisher
Scissor-tailed Flycatcher
Mangrove Swallow
Gray-breasted Martin
Rufous-naped Wren
White-throated Magpie-Jay

Specialties:

Wood Stork
Bare-throated Tiger-Heron

Magnificent Frigatebird

Wood Stork

Additional Sites

La Calera Private Reserve
(*Reserva Privada La Calera*)

The La Calera Private Reserve is located south of Granada, about fifteen minutes by car from the Marina Cocibolca in Asese. This site protects dry tropical forest, plus wetlands, lagoons, and hot springs. Several trails have been developed on the grounds that offer good birding opportunities. The wetlands and lagoons can be explored by kayak or canoe. They also offer horseback riding and other recreational activities.

The old ranch house is located on a hillside and provides a beautiful view of the islatas and Mombacho Volcano. Rooms and meals are available. Contact the reserve for reservations or more information.

Contact:

Phone: 2552-5858; 2228-2073 or 8425-1931
Email: gerencia@marinacocibolca.net or fcrnvm@ibw.com.ni
Website: www.mombacho.org or www.marinacocibolca.net

Mecatepe Lagoon Natural Reserve
(*Reserva Natural Lagunetas de Mecatepe*)

This reserve is located south of Mombacho Volcano and east of Lake Nicaragua. It lies in an area of relatively extensive dry tropical forest with several small lakes and ponds. Access is along a dirt road off of the Granada – Nandaime Highway. There are no accommodations on this site at this time and it is therefore a day-use area only. This is a newly established reserve with planned future improvements.

The Pacific Coast

Brown Pelican—Immature

Region 2
The Pacific Coast
The Western Edge

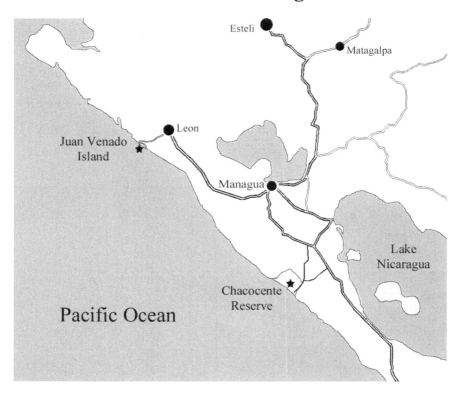

The Pacific Coast forms the entire western border of Nicaragua and attracts a wide variety of gulls, terns, herons, egrets, and other species. It also appears to contain a few important shorebird migration stop-over and wintering sites, although further surveys are needed. Much of the Pacific coast is difficult to access from land, but two sites in particular provide great birding opportunities in this region.

Nicaragua's extensive Pacific coast has few main roads leading to it and many of these connect to fishing villages, swimming beaches and surfer resorts. However, along its western boundary there are two interesting birding sites.

Not far from Managua lies Chacocente Wildlife Refuge. This site is only easily reached during the dry season, but in addition to the coastal habitat, it also protects the largest remaining tract of dry tropical forest in the country along with its associated wildlife.

One of Nicaragua's most important mangrove forests is found near the village of Las Penitas at Juan Venado Island. This is also one of the best places in Nicaragua to find Mangrove Warbler, a race of the Yellow Warbler. This site also contains a large nesting colony of herons, egrets and spoonbills and provides a feeding ground for a wide variety of birds.

The mangroves can be easily explored by boat or kayak, and it is possible to hike the uninhabited island itself as well. Juan Venado Island is a nesting site for Olive Ridley Turtles.

Shorebirds remain a rather poorly studied group of birds in Nicaragua and recent surveys are attempting to identify the most important sites and document shorebird populations. From preliminary surveys it appears that the Gulf of Fonseca attracts a significant population of shorebirds. Additional monitoring is needed, but this area may provide some good birding potential.

Two additional birding sites have been included in the Pacific Coast section of this book and while they are not located on the coast itself, they are most easily visited when traveling through this region. These include the Cosiguina Volcano and the San Cristobal and El Chonco Volcanoes. Both of these sites are located near the city of Chinandega and provide adventureous hikes on the volcanoes as well as birding on the forested slopes. These sites are among the more remote of Nicaragua's volancoes and are day-use areas only.

Chacocente Wildlife Refuge
(*Refugio de Vida Silvestre Escalante-Chacocente*)

Site Description:

The Escalante River-Chacocente Wildlife Refuge was established in 1983 to protect a large expanse of tropical dry forest (4,600 hectares or 11,350 acres) and an important sea turtle nesting beach. The refuge starts just south of the Escalante River, which protects this entire stretch of the river, and encompasses the surrounding forest and adjacent waters. Unlike U.S. national wildlife refuges, most of Nicaragua's protected areas are not owned by the government, but by private landowners. Four small communities of farmers live within Chacocente Wildlife Refuge.

Chacocente has about 8 km of coast along the Pacific Ocean with protected waters extending 5 km out to sea. The turtle nesting season runs from July to January, with upwards of 18,000 turtles coming here. Each turtle will nest 3 to 4 times per season, so this area has the potential to produce more than a million hatchlings per year.

Chacocente provides opportunities to observe birds along both the coast and the adjacent dry forest, making for some great birding potential. The surrounding uplands protect one of the largest remaining stands of tropical dry forest in Central America. The reserve features a long coastline with adjacent hills, and valleys that flood during the rainy season.

Directions:

Chacocente is located about three hours south of Managua by car. A dirt road leads to the research center at Chacocente and is accessible by truck and mini-bus during dry season (mid- November to May). During the rainy season this reserve is only accessible by 4x4 or horse and following heavy rains the rivers may be impassable for periods of time.

From Managua, take the Pan-American Highway south to Jinotepe. From here it will take about two hours to reach the reserve. Continue to Km 80 by the Ochomogo bridge. Turn right after the bridge and follow the dirt road to Salinas Grandes. Continue over the Nahualapa bridge for another 10 kilometers to the village of Astillero. About one km after the village you should find a sign for Chacocente. This marks the entrance to the reserve, although the research station is another 20 minutes from here through several river crossings.

An alternative route is as follows. From Managua, take the Pan-American Highway south and turn left into Santa Teresa. Continue through the town of Santa Teresa and after about 10 km take a left following the main road. The turn-off is before the town of La Conquista. Continue for approximately another 10 km and take another left onto another dirt road, always following the main roads. Follow this road to the end and turn right. About one km from this point you will come to the refuge.

Public Transportation: From Managua or Granada, take a bus to Nandaime and then transfer to a bus to El Astillero. It is also possible to arrange transportation from Jinotepe or Santa Teresa by the local cooperative. Cost for the van is $80 with a maximum of eight persons (cost is per vehicle).

Access/ Accommodations:

The Ministry of the Environment (MARENA) runs the research station. The accommodations at Chacocente are rustic. Food and housing are available at the biological station and in the nearby communities. Camping is also allowed within the reserve (about $2/night). Rooms average $5 per person and meals run from $3 to $5 each. Since food for guests needs to be brought in from Jinotepe, it is suggested that you make reservations at least three days in advance.

There is no running water in the cabins; the people living in the research center get their water from a traditional well that is located about a kilometer from the research center. Since there is no plumbing in the nature reserve one has to use buckets for showering and flushing.

Solar panels provide electricity for about 4 hours every night. There is an entrance fee to Chacocente Beach of $5 with extra charges for camping paid directly to MARENA (Ministry of Natural Resources of Nicaragua). There are also hotels in the towns of Astillero and Guasacate to the south of the reserve that are more comfortable and located only a short distance from the refuge.

Chacocente Wildlife Refuge

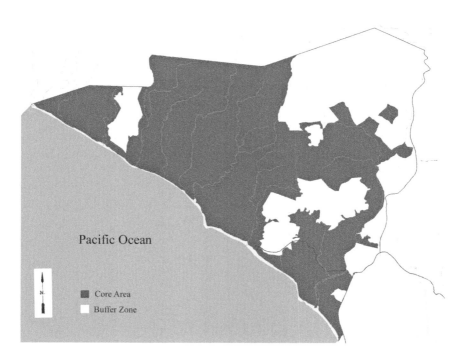

Contact:

Phone: 8603-3742 or 8481-1202
Email: info@chacocente-nicaragua.com
Website: www.chacocente-nicaragua.com

Trails/Guided Hikes:

Birding can be done on any of the area trails and backroads. A variety of guided hikes start from the research center. They average about 1 ½ hours and cost $10 per group up to five persons. Routes include:

Chacocente Turtle Nesting Beach
Los Tres Sombreros Trail and Vista al Refugio
River Escalante Trail, plus Ojos de Agua Overlook and Thermal Spring
Waterfall and Dry Forest Trail
El Guapinoles Overlook

Description of Birding Sites:

Birding is available along the beach of the Pacific coast for a variety of waterbirds. Hike the road in the reserve and any of the trails to access the tropical dry forest. Birding is also available on the Escalante and Acayo Rivers where you will find a gallery forest of the tallest trees in the reserve, as well as small stands of mangrove forest. Chacocente is also one of the few places to observe King Vulture in the Pacific region.

Orange-fronted Parakeet

Birds of Chacocente Reserve

Gray-headed Chachalaca
Blue-winged Teal
Magnificent Frigatebird
Neotropic Cormorant
Brown Pelican
Great Blue Heron
Great Egret
Snowy Egret
Little Blue Heron
Tricolored Heron
Cattle Egret
Green Heron
Roseate Spoonbill
Wood Stork
Osprey
Hook-billed Kite
Common Black-Hawk
Gray Hawk
Roadside Hawk
Northern Jacana
Black-necked Stilt
Spotted Sandpiper
Solitary Sandpiper
Lesser Yellowlegs
Red-billed Pigeon
White-winged Dove
Inca Dove
Common Ground-Dove
White-tipped Dove
Squirrel Cuckoo
Groove-billed Ani
Pacific Screech-Owl
Spectacled Owl
Mottled Owl
Common Nighthawk
Common Pauraque
Common Potoo
Long-billed Hermit
Magnificent Hummingbird
Plain-capped Starthroat

Ruby-throated Hummingbird
Canivet's Emerald
Steely-vented Hummingbird
Rufous-tailed Hummingbird
Cinnamon Hummingbird
Blue-throated Goldentail
Black-headed Trogon
Gartered Trogon
Elegant Trogon
Blue-crowned Motmot
Turquoise-browed Motmot
Ringed Kingfisher
Belted Kingfisher
Amazon Kingfisher
Green Kingfisher
American Pygmy Kingfisher
White-necked Puffbird
Emerald Toucanet
Collared Aracari
Hoffmann's Woodpecker
Lineated Woodpecker
Pale-billed Woodpecker
Olive-throated Parakeet
Orange-fronted Parakeet
Orange-chinned Parakeet
White-fronted Parrot
Mealy Parrot
Yellow-naped Parrot
Streaked-headed Woodcreeper
Common Tody-Flycatcher
Yellow-olive Flycatcher
Eastern Wood-Pewee
Tropical Pewee
Dusky-capped Flycatcher
Great Crested Flycatcher
Brown-crested Flycatcher
Streaked Flycatcher
Masked Tityra
Yellow-throated Vireo
Yellow-green Vireo

White-throated Magpie-Jay
Gray-breasted Martin
Bank Swallow
Cliff Swallow
Barn Swallow
Rufous-naped Wren
Spot-breasted Wren
Plain Wren
White-lored Gnatcatcher
Swainson's Thrush
Wood Thrush
Clay-colored Thrush

Worm-eating Warbler
Northern Waterthrush
Black-and-white Warbler
Tennessee Warbler
Yellow Warbler
Chestnut-sided Warbler
Buff-throated Saltator
Olive Sparrow
Summer Tanager
Scarlet Tanager
Melodious Blackbird
Montezuma Oropendola

Specialties:

Boat-billed Heron
Double-striped Thick-knee
Collared Plover
Mangrove Cuckoo

Lesser Ground-Cuckoo
Slate-headed Tody-Flycatcher
Nutting's Flycatcher

Magnificent Frigatebird

Juan Venado Island
(*Isla Juan Venado*)

Site Description:

Juan Venado Island is located south of the village of Las Peñitas. Juan Venado is a long, thin barrier island measuring 22 km in length and only ½ km wide and covers 2,934 hectares (7,250 acres). The island consists of tropical dry forest and mangroves and supports large nesting colonies of wading birds. On the Pacific coast side of Juan Venado Island, there is an important nesting site for Olive Ridley sea turtles. The shallow water separating the island from the mainland harbors crocodiles and caimans and provides a feeding ground for the many wading birds. More than 100 species of birds have been recorded here.

Juan Venado Island is uninhabited and has been set aside as a protected area for nesting Olive Ridley Turtle. The turtles are most often seen from August to December, and the best time to observe them is at night. The protected status of this island not only benefits the nesting turtles, but also serves as a sanctuary for nesting birds.

While Juan Venado Island falls under the jurisdiction of León, it is managed by a local NGO. The best way to explore the island is by motorboat or kayak. Las Peñitas is a small fishing village and any of the local fishermen can be contacted to take a boat ride among the shallow waters to explore the island. There also are some tour operators in the area and hotels also offer boat tours as well as kayak rentals.

Juan Venado Island is named for a local legend of a hunter who pursued deer (venado) in the area and therefore Isla Juan Venado translates as John Deer Island, having nothing to do with farming equipment.

Among the many species of birds that have been recorded here, a recent discovery of a Rufous-necked Wood Rail in late 2012 has been one of the most exciting observations.

Directions:

From León, take Highway 14 and follow signs to Poneloya. After 18 km you will approach the coast. Turn left just before Poneloya to reach Las Peñitas where you can arrange a boat tour or rent a kayak.

To approach the reserve from the south, turn west at Km 76 and drive 13 km on a rough dirt road toward Salinas Grande. At the salt ponds, go right and continue around the ponds. As you approach the coast, turn right and continue 2.2 km to reach the river and coast.

Public Transportation: To get to Las Peñitas, you can take a bus from León. It will take about 30 minutes to get there.

Access:

The best way to explore this area is by boat or kayak and paddle among the mangrove forest. There are small winding waterways where a variety of herons, egrets, cormorants, and other birds feed among the shallow water. However, these areas are only accessible during high tide, so be sure to check the tide schedule. A boat ride of about four hours will cost around $50 to $60, or $20 for a shorter trip. It is also possible to get out of a boat and walk the island.

Hours of operation:

This site can be covered as a day trip. Accommodations are available in Leon. Another option is to camp on the island. Local tour operators can help make arrangements for tents and guides.

Contact Information:

No prior arrangements are necessary. Simply check with the local fisherman or tour operators for rentals or guided boat tours of the area. Again, plan your visit to coincide with high tides so that you will have the greatest possible access to shallow water areas.

Yellow-crowned Night-Heron

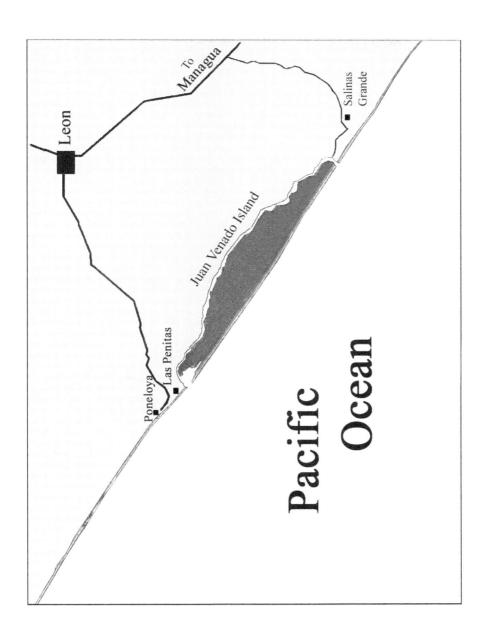

Pacific Ocean

Leon

To Managua

Salinas Grande

Juan Venado Island

Poneloya

Las Penitas

Description of Birding Sites:

The price for a three hour boat trip is around $45, and a longer trip is around $60. Boats can take up to 10 people and the price is per boat, so try to go with a larger group. Kayaks go for $10 per person at Hotel Barca de Oro, and $5.50 for hotel guests if you wish to explore the area alone. Be sure to bring sun screen and water, and try to go around sunrise or sunset, when the birds are most active.

Also, be sure to ask a guide or fishermen about the tide schedule. You can only freely navigate a boat or kayak between the shore and the island when the tide is high. During low tide you may get stranded, which means you will have to wait for hours before the water level rises again.

Common Birds:

About 10 species of herons and egrets can be found here.

Common birds include a variety of shorebirds, herons, terns and gulls.

Brown Pelican	Laughing Gull
Forster's Tern	Black Skimmer
Sandwich Tern	Belted Kingfisher
Caspian Tern	

Check the nearby shrubs for:

White-lored Gnatcatcher
Tropical Mockingbird
Stripe-headed Sparrow

Specialty Birds:

Roseate Spoonbill
White Ibis
Wood Stork
Boat-billed Heron
Rufous-necked Wood-Rail

Additional Sites

San Cristobal and El Chonco Volcanoes
(*Volcán San Cristóbal*)

The Las Banderas Forest is a 480 hectare site that is located between the foothills of the San Cristobal and El Chonco Volcanoes. It is located 15 kilometers northwest of the city of Chinandega and spans an elevation of 450 to 900 meters (1,475 to 2,950 feet) above sea level. The forest is a watershed management site for a number of nearby communities and is managed in cooperation with local partners and The Nature Conservancy.

Those wishing to hike this volcano can hire a guide for the three hour walk to the top of San Cristobal Volcano. There are several trails in the area, including the El Volcan trail which leads to the summit.

Contact: Phone: 2249 - 0499

Consiguina Volcano
(*Volcán Cosigüina*)

The Cosiguina Volcano is located in the far northwest corner of Nicaragua, around 70 kilometers north of Chinandega. It has a height of 859 meters (2,800 feet) with tree-covered slopes that reach most of the way to the Gulf of Fonseca and is a designated Important Bird Area.

Cosiguina Volcano experienced a major eruption in 1835 that blew apart a huge portion of the crater and hurled massive rocks to form islands in the Gulf of Fonseca. Ash fell as far away as Mexico City, nearly 900 miles distance. The volcano has been dormant since 1859 and in 1938 a crater lake formed within the volcano.

Hiking to the crater is not difficult since the slopes are quite gentle. A hiking trail starts at the MARENA office at the bottom of the volcano. The first half up the volcano is accessible by car. However, the dense trees and shrubs along this route keep the road quite narrow and may scratch the paint on a rental car, so be advised before driving on. From here, it will require about 90 minutes to reach the top.

The crater has a diameter of approximately 2 km, and the crater lake is located at a depth of 500 meters. It is no longer possible to hike to the lake as the only path leading into the crater was destroyed when a strong earthquake hit the area in 2001. From the top it is possible to see the Gulf of Fonseca, and Honduras and El Salvador beyond that.

The round-trip hike will take about three hours if you drive the first portion, or as much as eight hours if you start at the bottom of the volcano. There are a few hotels located close to the volcano for convenience and they can also help arrange transportation and a guide.

From Chinandega it is a two and a half hour drive to Consiguina. Follow the paved road from the city of El Viejo to the village of El Congo. From here take a dirt road to the town of Potosí, located on the northeast side of the Cosiguina Peninsula. It is recommended to take a four-wheel drive vehicle, particularly during the wet season. There are also buses leaving from Chinandega and El Viejo to Potosí, but not frequently. Ask about schedules at the bus terminal or in nearby hotels.

The forested area north of Consiguina Volcano is one of the last strongholds for the Scarlet Macaw in Nicaragua. Wetlands and lagoons in this area provide an important wintering site for a variety of ducks, including Blue-winged Teal, Northern Shoveler, Greater Scaup and resident Black-bellied Whistling-Duck and Muscovy Duck.

Beyond the peninsula lie three islands (Islotes de Cosigüina) that support Blue-footed and Brown Booby and provide an important nesting site for Bridled Tern. These islands are assessible by boat from Potosi. In the Gulf of Fonseca are extensive tidal wetlands and those converted to shrimp farms that attract migrant shorebirds, including Western Sandpiper, Dunlin and Red Knot.

South-Central Nicaragua

Keel-billed Toucan

Region 3
South-Central Nicaragua;
Islands and Rainforests

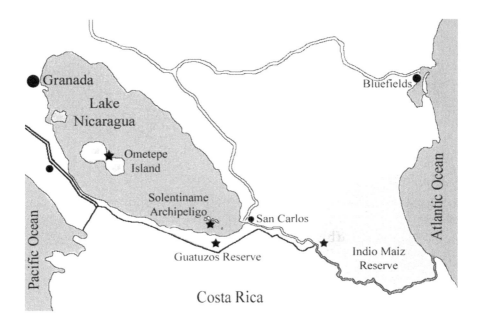

This region focuses on a number of sites in the Lake Nicaragua area, including Ometepe Island, the Solentiname Archipelago and the rainforests at Guatuzos and Indio Maiz. To bird these sites will require a trip of several days to allow for travel time to and from the site and sufficient time to cover the area. However, birders will be rewarded with an abundance of species of the wetland and rainforest habitats typical of the Costa Rican lowlands to the south.

The south-central region of Nicaragua is dominated by Lake Nicaragua and contains some amazing sites such as the magical island of Ometepe, which rises out of the lake forming the twin volcanic peaks. There are several interesting birding sites on Ometepe and the scenery created by the volcanic peaks is spectacular.

The Solentiname Archipelago provides another oasis for wildlife in this vast lake. Among this chain of islands, El Zapote Island is home to large colonies of thousands of nesting cormorants, herons, and spoonbills. The island lacks visitor services. Only day trips are possible, but it is located only about 15 km from San Carlos. There are also facilities on some of the other larger islands for those wishing to explore the area further.

There are several other sites in this region that offer great birding opportunities. Los Guatuzos is a natural reserve located on the south shore of Lake Nicaragua that stretches to the border with Costa Rica. Although difficult to access, the forest and wetland habitat is home to a wide range of birds. There is housing and a research center on-site with several trails in this section of the reserve. The remainder of the reserve can be explored by boat along the many rivers that course their way to Lake Nicaragua.

Another hotspot is the Indio Maíz Biological Reserve, which is one of Nicaragua's most impressive natural reserves. This area, measuring over 3,000 square kilometers, harbors some of Nicaragua's most spectacular wildlife, such as jaguars, pumas, tapirs and manatees. There are more than 400 species of birds known here, including the endangered Great Green Macaw and Great Curassow, making this one of the best birding sites in Nicaragua. The Indio Maíz Biological Reserve is situated in the southeastern corner of the country, bordering Costa Rica and the Caribbean Sea. Access is only possible by boat, and although it takes a little effort to reach this area, it is definitely worth it.

Aside from these featured birding sites, there are no additional sites described for this part of the country. However, the following sites will provide several days to a week or more of birding for anyone traveling to this region of the country.

Ometepe Island
(*Isla Ometepe*)

Site Description:

The name Ometepe comes from the Nahuatl language meaning two hills. Ometepe Island consists of two volcanos—Volcan Concepcion at 1,610 meters (5,282 feet) and Volcan Maderas, reaching to 1,394 meters (4,570 feet) above sea level. The lowlands have largely been developed for farming, but several areas provide good forest remnants and edge habitat, while the volcanos are covered with dense forest.

The forests covering the two volcanoes are largely inaccessible. There is a hiking trail to the top of each volcano, but it will require most of a day just to undertake the hike and birding can be difficult in the thick vegetation.

The island of Ometepe is on a dividing line between the wet tropical forests of the Atlantic Lowlands and the dry tropical forests of the Pacific Lowlands. This line falls directly between the two volcanoes. Southernmost Maderas Volcano is an extinct volcano and contains a crater lake. The slopes of Maderas are covered with plants more typical of the humid lowlands, and the upper elevations contain a cloud forest. The Concepcion Volcano is an active volcano whose slopes are covered with tropical dry forest vegetation. To date, a total of 148 species of birds have been recorded on Ometepe, with others yet to be discovered.

Ometepe Island

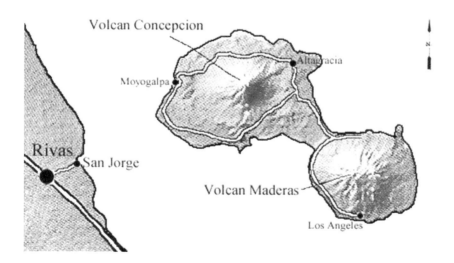

Directions:

To reach the island you will need to take a ferry. The Granada ferry leaves in the evening and is a long ride in the dark. The better way to Ometepe is to travel to Rivas and San Jorge. Here you can catch a ferry to Moyogalpa, which takes one hour. Several ferries make regular trips throughout the day, including those for passengers only and those transporting cars and trucks.

Access/Accommodations:

Ferries charge around $2 to $3 per person and $25 each way for a car and driver. Prices vary slightly among the different ferries. It is suggested to call ahead for reservations, particularly on weekends. There are places to stay in several of the towns on the island, as well as Villa Paraiso at Playa Santo Domingo, Charco Verde Lodge and Totoco Ecolodge among others.

Contact:

For ferry service schedules or reservations:
Phone: 8691-3669 or 2563-0665 or 8966-4978.
Website: www.ometepenicaragua.com

Description of Birding Sites:

General birding is available along the area roads and lakeshore as you travel around the island. Two protected areas are located near Playa Santo Domingo; Peña Inculta and the Rio Istian estuary. These reserves protect a dry tropical forest and a wetland and river estuary, respectively. On the southern shore of Concepcion lies Charco Verde Reserve. The most unique species occur on the slopes of the volcanos, particularly the cloud forest of Maderas Volcano. Each of these sites is covered in varying detail below.

Volcan Concepcion

Volcan Concepcion is the larger of the two volcanoes that make up Ometepe Island. Farmland and plantations cover the lower slopes, with extensive forest further up. The upper reaches are very steep and barren. The ascent is a 10-hour hike and due to its difficult access, this is more for adventurers than birders. Because of the limited trails, steep slopes, and volcanic activity, this remains a poorly surveyed area with many more bird species to be recorded.

Volcan Concepcion as seen from San Jorge.

Volcan Maderas

Volcan Maderas is not as tall or steep as Volcan Concepcion and is therefore somewhat more accessible. However, the hike up this volcano is a climb and still quite difficult. The main trail to the top starts at the village of Balgue and will require eight hours to complete the 4.5 km hike to the top and back. Once at the top, you can hike down to the crater lake.

The forest is quite dense most of the way, making birding a bit challenging through the foliage, and the thick cloud forest does not allow many views of the surrounding land. Also, like most of Nicaragua's volcanoes, clouds form around the upper reaches on most days. Still the area harbors a nice variety of bird species as you travel through the lower forest to the cloud forest above to ascend this spectacular volcano.

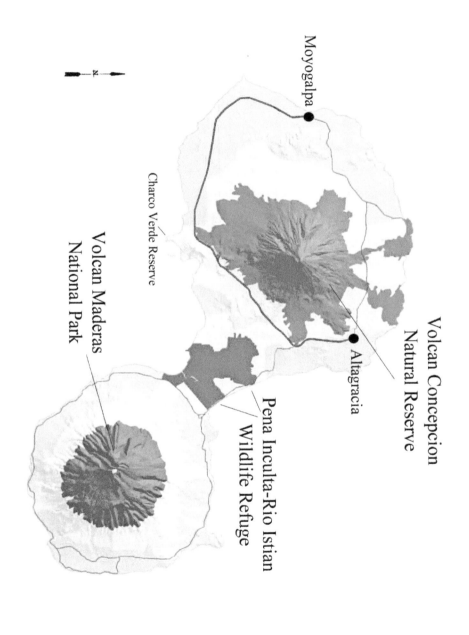

Moyogalpa

Charco Verde Reserve

Volcan Maderas
National Park

Volcan Concepcion
Natural Reserve

Altagracia

Pena Inculta-Rio Istian
Wildlife Refuge

104

Peña Inculta Reserve
(*Refugio de Vida Silvestre Peña Inculta*)

Peña Inculta and Rio Istian are ajoining reserves and often treated as one unit, but I have chosen to list them separately since they contain such different habitats. Peña Inculta is located adjacent to Playa Santo Domingo on the north side of the strip of land between the two volcanoes. This reserve protects some of the best dry tropical forest on Ometepe Island. There are a few small hotels in the area as Playa Domingo is one of the more popular beaches on Ometepe Island.

Peña Incluta has one hiking trail; a 1.2 km loop that leads through the forest. Birding can be done along the shore of the lake and forest edge or by hiking along this trail. This area is the most important site for Yellow-naped Parrots in the Pacific Lowlands with more than 300 parrots having been counted in this reserve.

Rio Istian
(*Refugio de Vida Silvestre Rio Istian*)

Rio Istian is a wetland and river delta formed where the rivers coming off of the volcanoes flows into Lake Nicaragua. For an island that is mostly farmland and forest, this is one of the few places where shorebirds and a variety of wading birds can be found on Ometepe Island. Tiger herons are common at this site among other species.

This reserve is located a short distance to the southeast of Peña Inculta Reserve. To get there, simply continue along the road that follows the shore of Playa Santo Domingo. Together these two sites make for good day trips for anyone birding Ometepe Island.

Peña Inculta Reserve
Hiking Trails

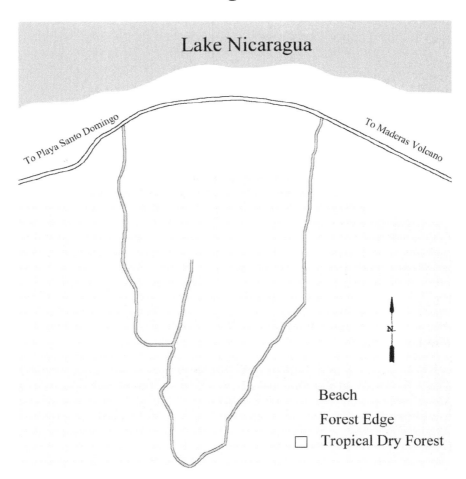

Charco Verde Private Reserve
(*Reserva Privada Charco Verde*)

Site Description:

Charco Verde is a protected area of dry tropical forest located on a point reaching out into Lake Nicaragua from the southern edge of Ometepe. This reserve protects a large forested area, plus a lagoon and beach. The lagoon, called Laguna Verde, is separated from the lake by a thin strip of land and provides good habitat for a variety of wetland birds. There is a hiking trail through the forest between the beach and reserve entrance.

Directions:

This reserve is located about 12 km from Moyogalpa on the main road to Altagracia. There is a sign along the road indicating the reserve. At the entrance of the reserve there is the Hotel Charco Verde where another beach is located. Enter Charco Verde at the hotel where information and accommodations are available. An entrance fee of less than one dollar is charged, which includes use of the beach and facilities.

Clay-colored Thrush

Birds of Ometepe Island

Black-bellied Whistling-Duck
Blue-winged Teal
Wood Stork
Magnificent Frigatebird
Anhinga
Brown Pelican
Bare-throated Tiger-Heron
Great Blue Heron
Great Egret
Snowy Egret
Little Blue Heron
Tricolored Heron
Cattle Egret
Green Heron
Black-crowned Night-Heron
Boat-billed Heron
White Ibis
Osprey
White-tailed Kite
Double-toothed Kite
Common Black-Hawk
Roadside Hawk
Gray Hawk
Sora
Limpkin
Northern Jacana
Black-necked Stilt
Spotted Sandpiper
Greater Yellowlegs
Laughing Gull
Caspian Tern
Red-billed Pigeon
Inca Dove
Common Ground-Dove
Ruddy Ground-Dove
Lesser Ground-Cuckoo
Barn Owl
Pacific Screech-Owl
Green-breasted Mango
Plain-capped Starthroat

Ruby-throated Hummingbird
Canivet's Emerald
White-bellied Emerald
Blue-tailed Hummingbird
Steely-vented Hummingbird
Rufous-tailed Hummingbird
Cinnamon Hummingbird
Blue-throated Goldentail
Black-headed Trogon
Gartered Trogon
Ringed Kingfisher
Belted Kingfisher
Green Kingfisher
Green-and-rufous Kingfisher
Hoffmann's Woodpecker
Barred Forest-Falcon
Crested Caracara
Peregrine Falcon
Pacific Parakeet
Crimson-fronted Parakeet
Orange-fronted Parakeet
Orange-chinned Parakeet
Brown-hooded Parrot
White-fronted Parrot
Mealy Parrot
Northern Beardless Tyrannulet
Greenish Elaenia
Mountain Elaenia
Ochre-bellied Flycatcher
Western Wood-Pewee
Eastern Wood-Pewee
Streaked Flycatcher
Yellow-bellied Flycatcher
Willow Flycatcher
Least Flycatcher
Dusky-capped Flycatcher
Nutting's Flycatcher
Great Crested Flycatcher
Brown-crested Flycatcher
Sulphur-bellied Flycatcher

Scissor-tailed Flycatcher
Masked Tityra
Rose-throated Becard
Warbling Vireo
Red-eyed Vireo
Philadelphia Vireo
Yellow-green Vireo
White-throated Magpie-Jay
Mangrove Swallow
Bank Swallow
Barn Swallow
Banded Wren
Rufous-and-white Wren
Plain Wren
Orange-billed Nightingale-Thrush
Swainson's Thrush
Wood Thrush
White-throated Thrush
Ovenbird
Worm-eating Warbler
Northern Waterthrush

Black-and-white Warbler
Prothonotary Warbler
Tennessee Warbler
Kentucky Warbler
American Redstart
Tropical Parula
Yellow Warbler
Chestnut-sided Warbler
Fan-tailed Warbler
Canada Warbler
Wilson's Warbler
Blue-gray Tanager
Buff-throated Saltator
Summer Tanager
Rose-breasted Grosbeak
Blue Grosbeak
Indigo Bunting
Painted Bunting
Dickcissel
Orchard Oriole
Baltimore Oriole

Specialties:

Crested Guan
Lesser Ground-Cuckoo
Purple-throated Mountain-gem
Plain-capped Starthroat
Blue-throated Goldentail

Red-lored Parrot
Yellow-naped Parrot
Three-wattled Bellbird
Orange-billed Nightingale-Thrush

Solentiname Archipelago
(*Archipielago Solentiname*)

Site Description:

The Solentiname Archipelago lies on the southern end of Lake Nicaragua and consists of a series of 36 volcanic islands. These islands vary in both size and vegetative cover. Since pre-Columbian times this chain of islands has been a sacred place for indigenous people as evidenced by the many petroglyphs with images of monkeys, parrots and humans. The Solentiname Islands lie in the transition zone between wet and dry tropical forests. A total of 76 species of birds have been recorded here. While not extremely diverse, the main attraction is the large colonies of nesting birds. The following is an overview of several of the major islands in this archipelago.

Mancarrón Island – Mancarrón is the main island with only some 200 people living here. This island measures 20 sq. km and is covered with lush vegetation. The village has two small stores that sell snacks and refreshments, and there are several artists' studios located here.

Local guides can be hired to hike the island. A popular destination is the overlook at Cerro Las Cuevas, which reaches to 260 meters (850 feet) and offers a great view of the other islands. This island is known for a type of palm tree (the mancarrón) that produces sweet palm wine.

San Fernando Island – Also known as La Isla Elvis Chavarría, this island is named after a young martyr killed during the revolution. It is the archipelago's second-biggest island and contains a sizeable community.

La Venada Island – Also called Isla Donald Guevara, this long, narrow island is known for an underwater cave, La Cueva del Duende.

This cave is of mythological importance to the Guatuzu tribe who believed that it leads to the underworld. It is located on the north side of the island and is only accessible by boat and during the dry season.

Mancarroncito Island – This is one of the archipelago's most undeveloped island. This highest peak reaches 100 meters (325 feet) and is covered in dense vegetation. This is a good place to search for forest birds, but it is advisable to go with a guide.

Zapote Island – This small island is perhaps the highlight of the archipelago. It is close to San Carlos and has been designated as a bird refuge. The island supports a colony of some 20,000 nesting birds, including herons, egrets, spoonbills, and storks.

Directions:

It will require a boat trip from San Carlos to reach these islands. Boats depart San Carlos at 3:00 pm and return from the islands at 9:00 am. It will take about 45 minutes to an hour to reach the islands. Cost for the boat is $10.

Accommodations:

There are places to stay on both Mancarrón and San Fernando Island and a lodge has been developed on Mancarroncito Island.

Description of Birding Sites:

The best birding is to visit the rookery sites on Isla El Zapote and watch birds as you cruise around by boat. Forest birds can be found along the trails on the larger islands as well as watching from the transport to and from the islands.

Common Birds of the Area:

Neotropic Cormorant, Bare-throated Tiger-Heron, White Ibis, Great Egret, Green Heron, Roseate Spoonbill and other colonial nesting species.

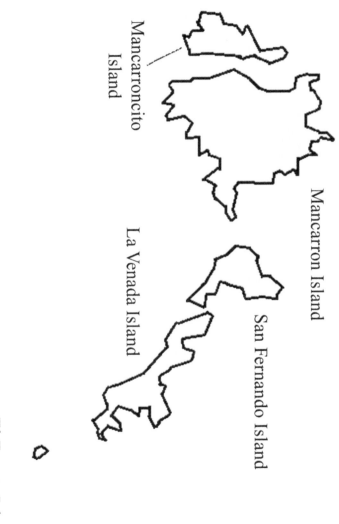

Mancarroncito Island

Mancarron Island

La Venada Island

San Fernando Island

Solentiname Islands

El Zapote Island

Los Guatuzos Wildlife Refuge
(*Refugio de Vida Silvestre Los Guatuzos*)

Site Description:

Located on the southern shore of Lake Nicaragua and extending all the way to the border with Costa Rica, the Los Guatuzos Wildlife Refuge is a 437 sq km (108,000 acres) reserve covering most of southeastern shores of Lake Nicaragua. Guatuzos is a protected wetland and wildlife reserve inhabited by 1,700 fisherman and subsistence farmers in 11 small communities and was dedicated as a Ramsar Site in 1997. This site includes tropical dry forest, tropical wet forest (rainforest) and extensive wetlands. A total of 389 species of birds have been recorded here.

More than a dozen rivers run through Guatuzos Reserve with the most popular for wildlife viewing being the Rio Papaturro, which drains the slopes of Costa Rica's northern volcanoes. Much of the area becomes flooded during the rainy season. The reserve is named after the community of Los Guatuzos, taken from an indigenous tribe that once lived here.

Directions/Access:

From the west dock in San Carlos, boats leave for Papaturro at 7:00 am Monday, Tuesday and Thursday. The four hour trip costs C$100, or about $4 per person. The same boat returns to San Carlos the day after arriving, leaving Papaturro at 7:00 am.

Another boat to Papaturro leaves San Carlos on Tuesdays, Wednesdays and Fridays at 9 a.m., returning to San Carlos Mondays, Tuesdays and Thursdays at 9 a.m. The trip is about 2 hours and costs $4.50 per person.

Access/accommodations:

Los Guatuzos Ecological Center is located 40 km from San Carlos, close to the Papaturro River within the Los Guatuzos Reserve. The Center is devoted to the management of the reserve and conducts research and workshops with ecologists and students.

The Ecological Center has two large rooms with eight beds in each at $11 per night, plus campgrounds (tents and sleeping bags available for rent). Arrange meals in advance in the nearby village for about $4. A variety of tours is available and cost about $11 per person. Another option is to stay at the Esperanza Verde Natural Reserve (see next section), which is also part of Los Guatuzos.

Contact Information:

Fundacion de Amigos del Rio San Juan (Fundar) 2265 0807;
2265-1821
Phone: 2270-5434 (Managua) or 583-0139 (San Carlos)
Email: centro.ecologico@fundar.org.ni
Information: info@losguatuzos.com
Reservations: reservacion@losguatuzos.com
Websites: www.fundar.org.ni
www.losguatuzos.com

The Managua office may be contacted at:
Telephone: 2270-3561
E-mail: nicaragua@tierra-org
Website: www.tierra.org

Trails:

There is a $6 entrance fee, which also includes a tour of the grounds. A variety of guided tours leave from the Ecological Center, including a butterfly farm, a caiman nursery, and a turtle nursery, as well as an orchid garden and heliconia garden.

There are several short trails and a wobbly system of canopy bridges within this part of the reserve. A 150-meter suspension bridge overlooks a wetland and forest edge. There is a $10 fee to access the canopy walk.

A variety of birdwatching tours are available through the Ecological Center. Short trips include a boat trip of three kilometers followed by a hike for $25/person. Longer trips continue to the shore of Lake Nicaragua and the Zapote River for a cost of $138/group. Kayaks can also be rented for about $15 per person.

Guided tours are conducted on the trails, but these can be hiked alone to watch birds. Take either the El Peresozo Trail or the Las Guatuzas Trails. A trail fee of $5.00 per person is charged by the reserve. The staff also conducts night hikes of about 1½ hours at $11 per person.

Description of Birding Sites:

Birding can be done from any of the trails located at the center or by boat. The many rivers that traverse this reserve provide abundant opportunities for birding along these waterways. All arrangements should be made with the office at the Ecological Center.

Birds of Los Guatuzos

Great Tinamou
Little Tinamou
Black-bellied Whistling-Duck
Fulvous Whistling-Duck
Muscovy Duck
American Wigeon
Blue-winged Teal
Greater Scaup
Lesser Scaup
Gray-headed Chachalaca
Least Grebe
Pied-billed Grebe
Wood Stork
Magnificent Frigatebird
Neotropic Cormorant
Anhinga
Brown Pelican
Least Bittern
Rufescent Tiger-Heron
Bare-throated Tiger-Heron
Great Blue Heron
Great Egret
Snowy Egret
Little Blue Heron
Tricolored Heron
Reddish Egret
Cattle Egret
Green Heron
Black-crowned Night-Heron
Yellow-crowned Night-Heron
White Ibis
Glossy Ibis
Roseate Spoonbill
Lesser Yellow-headed Vulture
Osprey
White-tailed Kite
Hook-billed Kite
Gray-headed Kite
Swallow-tailed Kite
Snail Kite

Mississippi Kite
Plumbeous Kite
Tiny Hawk
Common Black-Hawk
Great Black-Hawk
Roadside Hawk
Harris's Hawk
White-tailed Hawk
White Hawk
Semiplumbeous Hawk
Broad-winged Hawk
Gray Hawk
Short-tailed Hawk
Swainson's Hawk
Zone-tailed Hawk
Gray-necked Wood-Rail
Purple Gallinule
Limpkin
Double-striped Thick-knee
Collared Plover
Wilson's Plover
Killdeer
Black-necked Stilt
Northern Jacana
Spotted Sandpiper
Solitary Sandpiper
Least Sandpiper
Pectoral Sandpiper
Wilson's Snipe
Laughing Gull
Royal Tern
Pale-vented Pigeon
Scaled Pigeon
Red-billed Pigeon
Short-billed Pigeon
White-winged Dove
Inca Dove
Plain-breasted Ground-Dove
Ruddy Ground-Dove
Blue Ground-Dove

White-tipped Dove
Gray-chested Dove
Squirrel Cuckoo
Striped Cuckoo
Groove-billed Ani
Barn Owl
Vermiculated Screech-Owl
Spectacled Owl
Central American Pygmy-Owl
Mottled Owl
Black-and-white Owl
Short-tailed Nighthawk
Lesser Nighthawk
Common Pauraque
Great Potoo
White-collared Swift
Vaux's Swift
Gray-rumped Swift
Lesser Swallow-tailed Swift
Bronzy Hermit
Long-billed Hermit
Band-tailed Barbthroat
Plain-capped Starthroat
Blue-chested Hummingbird
Steely-vented Hummingbird
Green-breasted Mango
Ruby-throated Hummingbird
Rufous-tailed Hummingbird
Cinnamon Hummingbird
Canivet's Emerald
Stripe-tailed Hummingbird
Violet-crowned Woodnymph
Scaly-breasted Hummingbird
Blue-throated Goldentail
Slaty-tailed Trogon
Black-headed Trogon
Black-throated Trogon
Gartered Trogon
Blue-crowned Motmot
Ringed Kingfisher
Belted Kingfisher

Amazon Kingfisher
Green Kingfisher
Green-and-rufous Kingfisher
American Pygmy Kingfisher
White-necked Puffbird
White-whiskered Puffbird
White-fronted Nunbird
Collared Aracari
Black-mandibled Toucan
Keel-billed Toucan
Olivaceous Piculet
Black-cheeked Woodpecker
Hoffmann's Woodpecker
Smoky-brown Woodpecker
Golden-olive Woodpecker
Cinnamon Woodpecker
Lineated Woodpecker
Pale-billed Woodpecker
Collared Forest-Falcon
Crested Caracara
Laughing Falcon
Bat Falcon
Crimson-fronted Parakeet
Olive-throated Parakeet
Orange-fronted Parakeet
Orange-chinned Parakeet
Brown-hooded Parrot
White-crowned Parrot
White-fronted Parrot
Red-lored Parrot
Mealy Parrot
Yellow-naped Parrot
Great Antshrike
Barred Antshrike
Western Slaty Antshrike
Streak-crowned Antvireo
White-flanked Antwren
Slaty Antwren
Dot-winged Antwren
Dusky Antbird
Bare-crowned Antbird

Chestnut-backed Antbird
Bicolored Antbird
Spotted Antbird
Black-faced Antthrush
Tawny-throated Leaftosser
Scaly-throated Leaftosser
Olivaceous Woodcreeper
Long-tailed Woodcreeper
Plain-brown Woodcreeper
Tawny-winged Woodcreeper
Ruddy Woodcreeper
Wedge-billed Woodcreeper
Northern Barred Woodcreeper
Black-striped Woodcreeper
Streaked-headed Woodcreeper
Plain Xenops
Buff-throated Foliage-gleaner
Ruddy Foliage-gleaner
Yellow-bellied Tyrannulet
Northern Beardless Tyrannulet
Yellow Tyrannulet
Greenish Elaenia
Yellow-bellied Elaenia
Ochre-bellied Flycatcher
Paltry Tyrannulet
Northern Bentbill
Slate-headed Tody-Flycatcher
Common Tody-Flycatcher
Yellow-olive Flycatcher
Yellow-margined Flycatcher
Royal Flycatcher
Olive-sided Flycatcher
Eastern Wood-Pewee
Tropical Pewee
Yellow-bellied Flycatcher
Acadian Flycatcher
Alder Flycatcher
White-throated Flycatcher
Least Flycatcher
Yellowish Flycatcher
Black Phoebe
Long-tailed Tyrant

Bright-rumped Attila
Rufous Mourner
Dusky-capped Flycatcher
Nutting's Flycatcher
Great Crested Flycatcher
Brown-crested Flycatcher
Boat-billed Flycatcher
Gray-capped Flycatcher
White-ringed Flycatcher
Streaked Flycatcher
Sulphur-bellied Flycatcher
Piratic Flycatcher
Eastern Kingbird
Scissor-tailed Flycatcher
Fork-tailed Flycatcher
Rufous Piha
Three-wattled Bellbird
Blue-crowned Manakin
White-collared Manakin
Red-capped Manakin
Black-crowned Tityra
Masked Tityra
White-winged Becard
Yellow-throated Vireo
Philadelphia Vireo
Red-eyed Vireo
Yellow-green Vireo
Tawny-crowned Greenlet
Lesser Greenlet
White-throated Magpie-Jay
Brown Jay
Northern Rough-winged Swallow
Southern Rough-winged Swallow
Gray-breasted Martin
Mangrove Swallow
Bank Swallow
Barn Swallow
Cliff Swallow
Nightingale Wren
House Wren
Band-backed Wren
Spot-breasted Wren

118

Black-throated Wren
Rufous-and-white Wren
Stripe-breasted Wren
Plain Wren
Bay Wren
White-breasted Wood-Wren
Tawny-faced Gnatwren
Long-billed Gnatwren
Tropical Gnatcatcher
Black-headed Nightingale-Thrush
Gray-cheeked Thrush
Swainson's Thrush
Wood Thrush
Clay-colored Thrush
White-throated Thrush
Gray Catbird
Ovenbird
Worm-eating Warbler
Louisiana Waterthrush
Northern Waterthrush
Golden-winged Warbler
Black-and-white Warbler
Prothonotary Warbler
Tennessee Warbler
Common Yellowthroat
Olive-crowned Yellowthroat
Gray-crowned Yellowthroat
Mourning Warbler
Kentucky Warbler
Hooded Warbler
American Redstart
Cerulean Warbler
Tropical Parula
Bay-breasted Warbler
Blackburnian Warbler
Yellow Warbler
Chestnut-sided Warbler
Black-throated Blue Warbler
Townsend's Warbler
Rufous-capped Warbler
Canada Warbler
Yellow-breasted Chat

Gray-headed Tanager
White-shouldered Tanager
Song Wren
Tawny-crested Tanager
Palm Tanager
Golden-hooded Tanager
Blue Dacnis
Shining Honeycreeper
Red-legged Honeycreeper
Green Honeycreeper
Blue-black Grassquit
White-collared Seedeater
Yellow-bellied Seedeater
Ruddy-breasted Seedeater
Thick-billed Seed-Finch
Bananaquit
Yellow-faced Grassquit
Grayish Saltator
Buff-throated Saltator
Black-headed Saltator
Orange-billed Sparrow
Black-striped Sparrow
Summer Tanager
Scarlet Tanager
Western Tanager
Red-throated Ant-Tanager
Carmiol's Tanager
Slate-colored Grosbeak
Black-faced Grosbeak
Rose-breasted Grosbeak
Blue-black Grosbeak
Indigo Bunting
Painted Bunting
Red-winged Blackbird
Eastern Meadowlark
Bronzed Cowbird
Giant Cowbird
Orchard Oriole
Yellow-tailed Oriole
Spot-breasted Oriole
Baltimore Oriole
Yellow-billed Cacique

Scarlet-rumped Cacique
Chestnut-headed Oropendola
Montezuma Oropendola
Scrub Euphonia

Yellow-crowned Euphonia
Yellow-throated Euphonia
Olive-backed Euphonia
White-vented Euphonia

Specialties:

Slaty-breasted Tinamou
Great Curassow
Jabiru
Pinnated Bittern
Fasciated Tiger-Heron
Striated Heron
Agami Heron
Boat-billed Heron
Green Ibis
Crested Eagle
Black-and-white Hawk-Eagle
Black-collared Hawk
Ruddy Crake
White-throated Crake
Gray-breasted Crake
Spotted Rail
Sungrebe

Ruddy Quail-Dove
White-necked Jacobin
Bronze-tailed Plumeleteer
Rufous Motmot
Pied Puffbird
Yellow-eared Toucanet
Rufous-winged Woodpecker
Chestnut-colored Woodpecker
Fasciated Antshrike
Slaty Spinetail
Stub-tailed Spadebill
Golden-crowned Spadebill
Speckled Mourner
Snowy Cotinga
Purple-throated Fruitcrow
Bare-necked Umbrellabird
Nicaraguan Seed-Finch
Nicaraguan Grackle

Bananaquit

Esperanza Verde Reserve
(*Reserva Esperanza Verde*)

Site Description:

Also within Guatuzos Reserve is the 4,000-hectare (10,000 acre) Esperanza Verde Private Reserve, located along the Rio Frio. This reserve is only 30 minutes from San Carlos by boat and therefore makes for a good day trip or longer. It was established as an effort to reforest and protect the overgrazed watershed of the Rio Frio and Rio San Juan.

Directions:

The only way to get to this reserve is by boat from San Carlos. Leaving San Carlos, boats cross the San Juan River and then enter the Rio Frio, traveling another 20 minutes to reach the lodge.

You will need to take a Los Chiles-bound boat from the port in San Carlos and ask to be dropped off at Esperanza Verde. The boats leave daily at 10.30 a.m. and return to San Carlos around 4:00 p.m.

Access/Accommodations:

When you arrive at the dock for Esperanza Verde and the military post, walk ½ km downstream to the Konrad Lorenz Environmental Education Center (Centro de Interpretación Ambiental Konrad Lorenz). Day visits to the reserve charge a $1 entrance fee. Guided tours cost $5 to $10 for the different available tours.

The reserve has an eight room lodge with 20 beds (double, triple and multiple) and restaurant service. The cost is $40 per person, and includes housing, three meals and trail fees. A day trip from San Carlos costs $25 per person and includes transportation, entrance fee, and lunch (minimum of two people). The center includes an auditorium with capacity for up to 60 people for courses, workshops, and retreats.

Contact: www.fundeverde.org/ or
reservaesperanzaverde.blogspot.com/

Trails:

The reserve provides horseback riding, canoes, and hikes along the trails through the forest. From the lodge, a 40-minute walk up the road leads to dense rainforest. The roadside edge and forest provide birding potential. There are three trails in the reserve and several trips by water.

Mirador Trail (1km—20 minutes)
This trail leads to an observation deck with an overlook of a wetland.

The Peter Trail (2 km—40 minutes)
This trail follows the river through lowland forest. The reserve conducts tours here focusing on tropical trees and agriculture.

Coralillo Trail (5 km—3 hours)
The trail winds through primary rainforest with good habitat for forest interior species. Trails can be muddy following heavy rain.

La Esquina del Lago

Another option for longer trips to Los Guatuzos Refuge is to stay at the lodge at La Esquina del Lago. This lodge sits on the lake, across from San Carlos at the mouth of Río Frío. The focus of many of their tours is fishing, but birding trips can be done from here.

The lodge offers large rooms with private bathrooms, for $30 (single) to $50 (double), or $80 as a package with three meals. Tours of Los Guatuzos can be done alone or with a guide in this section of the reserve.

Contact:
Tel: 8849-0600,
E-mail: riosanjuan@)racsa.co.cr
Website: www.nicaraguafishing.com or www.riosanjuan.info.

Indio Maiz Biological Reserve – Bartola (*Reserve Biologico Indio Maíz*)

Site Description:

The Indio Maiz Biological Reserve is considered one of the most wild and pristine sites in Nicaragua. The area is located in the southeast corner of the country, bordering the San Juan River. The reserve encompasses 3,618 km² (894,000 acres) between the Indio and Maiz rivers, and provides essential habitat to a wide variety of rainforest animals.

A vast portion of this reserve is closed to public access and the Ministry of Natural Resources (MARENA) does not allow people to enter the reserve in most places. There are, however, two areas in this remote region where visitors can explore Indio Maiz; at Bartola on the west side and San Juan del Nicaragua on the Caribbean side (see next section).

Directions:

The Bartola River forms the western border of the Indio Maiz Reserve to where it flows into the San Juan River. Bartola is located only 6 km downstram from the historic town of El Castillo. Visitors can arrange day trips to the reserve from here or Sabalos Lodge by traveling down the San Juan River, or stay at the Bartola Lodge across the river from the reserve.

A guide is necessary to enter the reserve, and visitors can hire a guide and arrange transportation in town or at the lodges. It is also possible to hire one of the guards from MARENA who are stationed at the entrance of the reserve.

The reserve is open at Bartola between 6:00 am and 2:00 pm for day trips. Boats leave San Carlos at 1:30 pm and 2:30 pm, departing from Bodega El Puerto. It will take about three hours to arrive at Bartola. Considering the travel time to reach this remote reserve, visitors should plan to stay in the area for several days.

Access/accommodations:

Lodging is available at Sabalos Lodge or at Bartola Lodge. Bartola Lodge offers food and lodging on the edge of the reserve. The lodge has 11 rooms and costs about $50 per person, depending on group size. They also offer half day tours of about 6 hours to the Sarnosa River, which is located about 30 to 45 minutes down the San Juan River. The following trail information is provided for the Bartola Lodge area.

Contact:

Phone: 8376-6979 or 8873-8586 (Managua office)
Email: refugiobartola@yahoo.com
Website: www.refugiobartola.com
www.sabaloslodge.com

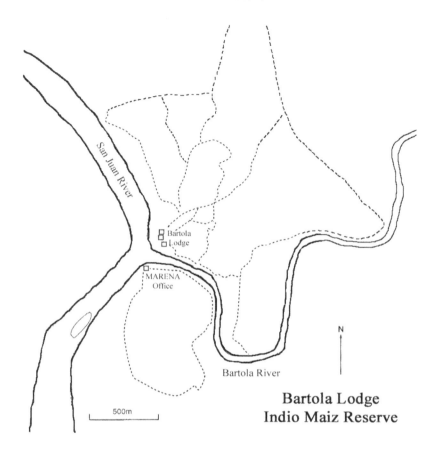

**Bartola Lodge
Indio Maiz Reserve**

Trails:

Within the reserve there is a 2 km (2.5 hours) loop trail that begins at the MARENA office at the confluence of the Bartola and San Juan Rivers. A series of loop trails have been developed on the north side of the river at the Bartola Lodge. All of these trails can be very muddy after the frequent rain, however, the lodge provides rubber boots for convenience.

Description of Birding Sites:

The hiking trails go through lowland forest near the rivers while others at Bartola Lodge extend inland into secondary and primary forest. Walking any of these trails can provide abundant opportunities for birding.

From Bartola, there are two river trips that can be undertaken providing excellent birding and a great jungle experience. A trip up the Bartola River can be done from the Bartola Lodge, which provides boats and guides. Likewise, arrangements can be made for a trip up the Sarnosa River, which is located about 30 minutes down the San Juan River from here. With these options and the potential for seeing a great abundance of birds, plan for a trip of at least three days here.

Birds of the Area:

More than 400 species of birds have been recorded at Bartola. This is the best place in the country to see Great Green Macaw, plus a number of other species known to Costa Rica that reach their northern limit here.

Boat-billed Heron

Birds of Indio Maiz – Bartola

Great Tinamou
Little Tinamou
Muscovy Duck
Blue-winged Teal
Gray-headed Chachalaca
Neotropic Cormorant
Anhinga
Rufescent Tiger-Heron
Great Blue Heron
Great Egret
Snowy Egret
Little Blue Heron
Tricolored Heron
Cattle Egret
Green Heron
Black-crowned Night-Heron
Roseate Spoonbill
Wood Stork
Black Vulture
Turkey Vulture
Osprey
Gray-headed Kite
Hook-billed Kite
Swallow-tailed Kite
Plumbeous Kite
Semiplumbeous Hawk
White Hawk
Great Black-Hawk
Gray Hawk
Short-tailed Hawk
Red-tailed Hawk
Roadside Hawk
Broad-winged Hawk
Swainson's Hawk
Black Hawk-Eagle
Laughing Falcon
Barred Forest-Falcon
Peregrine Falcon
Bat Falcon
White-throated Crake

Gray-necked Wood-Rail
Purple Gallinule
Sungrebe
Killdeer
Northern Jacana
Spotted Sandpiper
Royal Tern
Pale-vented Pigeon
Scaled Pigeon
Red-billed Pigeon
Short-billed Pigeon
Mourning Dove
Ruddy Ground-Dove
Blue Ground-Dove
White-tipped Dove
Gray-chested Dove
Olive-backed Quail-Dove
Ruddy Quail-Dove
Crimson-fronted Parakeet
Olive-throated Parakeet
Orange-chinned Parakeet
Brown-hooded Parrot
White-crowned Parrot
Red-lored Parrot
Mealy Parrot
Squirrel Cuckoo
Striped Cuckoo
Groove-billed Ani
Vermiculated Screech-Owl
Spectacled Owl
Central American Pygmy-Owl
Short-tailed Nighthawk
Common Nighthawk
Common Pauraque
Chuck-will's-widow
Great Potoo
Common Potoo
White-collared Swift
Gray-rumped Swift
Lesser Swallow-tailed Swift

Band-tailed Barbthroat
Long-billed Hermit
Stripe-throated Hermit
Scaly-breasted Hummingbird
White-necked Jacobin
Green-breasted Mango
Violet-headed Hummingbird
Black-crested Coquette
Violet-crowned Woodnymph
Blue-chested Hummingbird
Rufous-tailed Hummingbird
Bronze-tailed Plumeleteer
Purple-crowned Fairy
Gartered Trogon
Black-throated Trogon
Slaty-tailed Trogon
Ringed Kingfisher
Belted Kingfisher
Amazon Kingfisher
Green Kingfisher
American Pygmy Kingfisher
White-necked Puffbird
Pied Puffbird
White-whiskered Puffbird
White-fronted Nunbird
Great Jacamar
Collared Aracari
Yellow-eared Toucanet
Keel-billed Toucan
Black-mandibled Toucan
Black-cheeked Woodpecker
Cinnamon Woodpecker
Chestnut-colored Woodpecker
Lineated Woodpecker
Pale-billed Woodpecker
Slaty Spinetail
Buff-throated Foliage-gleaner
Plain Xenops
Scaly-throated Leaftosser
Plain-brown Woodcreeper
Wedge-billed Woodcreeper
Northern Barred Woodcreeper

Cocoa Woodcreeper
Black-striped Woodcreeper
Spotted Woodcreeper
Streaked-headed Woodcreeper
Fasciated Antshrike
Great Antshrike
Barred Antshrike
Western Slaty Antshrike
Streak-crowned Antvireo
Checker-throated Antwren
White-flanked Antwren
Dot-winged Antwren
Dusky Antbird
Chestnut-backed Antbird
Spotted Antbird
Black-faced Antthrush
Yellow Tyrannulet
Yellow-bellied Elaenia
Ochre-bellied Flycatcher
Paltry Tyrannulet
Black-capped Pygmy Tyrant
Northern Bentbill
Common Tody-Flycatcher
Yellow-olive Flycatcher
Yellow-margined Flycatcher
Golden-crowned Spadebill
Ruddy-tailed Flycatcher
Sulphur-bellied Flycatcher
Tawny-chested Flycatcher
Tropical Pewee
Yellow-bellied Flycatcher
Least Flycatcher
Bright-rumped Attila
Rufous Mourner
Dusky-capped Flycatcher
Great Crested Flycatcher
Boat-billed Flycatcher
Gray-capped Flycatcher
White-ringed Flycatcher
Piratic Flycatcher
Rufous Piha
White-ruffed Manakin

128

White-collared Manakin
Red-capped Manakin
Black-crowned Tityra
Masked Tityra
Northern Shiffornis
Cinnamon Becard
White-winged Becard
Yellow-throated Vireo
Philadelphia Vireo
Red-eyed Vireo
Yellow-green Vireo
Tawny-crowned Greenlet
Lesser Greenlet
Green Shike-Vireo
Gray-breasted Martin
Mangrove Swallow
Blue-and-white Swallow
No.Rough-winged Swallow
Bank Swallow
Cliff Swallow
Barn Swallow
Black-throated Wren
Bay Wren
Plain Wren
House Wren
White-breasted Wood-Wren
Tawny-faced Gnatwren
Long-billed Gnatwren
Tropical Gnatcatcher
Swainson's Thrush
Wood Thrush
Gray Catbird
Golden-winged Warbler
Tennessee Warbler
Yellow Warbler
Chestnut-sided Warbler
Black-and-white Warbler
Northern Waterthrush
Louisiana Waterthrush
Kentucky Warbler
Mourning Warbler
Olive-crowned Yellowthroat

Gray-crowned Yellowthroat
Hooded Warbler
Canada Warbler
Buff-rumped Warbler
Bananaquit
Carmiol's Tanager
White-shouldered Tanager
Tawny-crested Tanager
Red-throated Ant-tanager
Summer Tanager
Scarlet Tanager
Crimson-collared Tanager
Passerini's Tanager
Palm Tanager
Bay-headed Tanager
Golden-hooded Tanager
Blue Dacnis
Green Honeycreeper
Shining Honeycreeper
Red-legged Honeycreeper
Blue-black Grassquit
Variable Seedeater
Nicaraguan Seed-Finch
Thick-billed Seed-Finch
Orange-billed Sparrow
Black-striped Sparrow
Grayish Saltator
Buff-throated Saltator
Slate-colored Grosbeak
Black-faced Grosbeak
Blue-black Grosbeak
Indigo Bunting
Red-winged Blackbird
Bronzed Cowbird
Giant Cowbird
Yellow-tailed Oriole
Baltimore Oriole
Yellow-billed Cacique
Chestnut-headed Oropendola
Montezuma Oropendola
Yellow-crowned Euphonia
Olive-backed Euphonia

Specialty Birds of the Area:

Slaty-breasted Tinamou
Great Curassow
Spotted Wood-Quail
Rufous-fronted Wood-Quail
Agami Heron
Boat-billed Heron
Green Ibis
Jabiru
King Vulture
Crested Eagle
Harpy Eagle
Great Green Macaw
Sunbittern
Crimson-fronted Parakeet
Blue-headed Parrot

Rufous-vented Ground-Cuckoo
Crested Owl
Rufous Nightjar
Ocellated Poorwill
Snowcap
Rufous-winged Woodpecker
Bicolored Antbird
Ocellated Antbird
Streak-chested Antpitta
Rufous Motmot
Broad-billed Motmot
Speckled Mourner
Snowy Cotinga
Purple-throated Fruitcrow
Bare-necked Umbrellabird
Scarlet-rumped Cacique

White-whiskered Puffbird

The Atlantic Lowlands

Limpkin

Region 4
The Atlantic Lowlands;
Rainforests and Coast

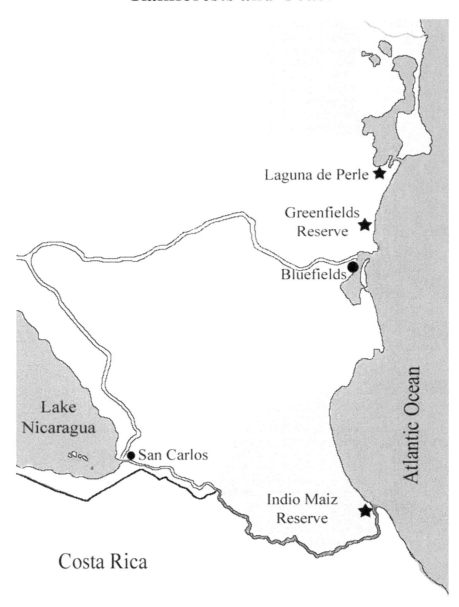

Laguna de Perle ★

Greenfields
Reserve ★

Bluefields ●

Atlantic Ocean

Lake
Nicaragua

● San Carlos

Indio Maiz
Reserve ★

Costa Rica

The Atlantic Lowlands extend along the entire eastern coast of Nicaragua and well inland. Most of this region is dominated by wet tropical forest, with an extensive network of rivers that wind their way toward the Caribbean. The coast is a mix of wetlands, estuaries, freshwater lagoons, and mangrove forests, as well as sand-washed beaches.

Added to this diversity, there are a number of off-shore islands that provide nesting sites for birds. The pelagic zone beyond Nicaragua's shores is poorly surveyed for birds, and it is likely that the country's list of birds will expand as more surveys are conducted and records added.

Because much of the coast is a low-lying rainforest, there are few settlements and sparse roads in this part of the country. Travel is confined to air travel and along the few roads that traverse the area, while the waterways provide access to much of the region. As a result, there are only three featured sites in this vast region.

The expansive Indio Maiz Reserve can be accessed from the town of San Juan de Nicaragua on the east. Farther up the coast, Greenfields Private Reserve and Laguna de Perle provide two other sites for birdwatchers. To reach these sites will require a trip of several days to allow for travel time to and from the site plus sufficient time to cover the area to observe birds.

There are other reserves in this region, including Wawashang Reserve, which is adjacent to Laguna de Perle and the Bosawas Biosphere Reserve, which is the largest rainforest reserve in Central America. Both of these sites are wild and difficult to penetrate but provide expansive habitat for resident and migrant birds.

One other additional site is listed at the end of this section. The Corn Islands are easily reached by air from Managua and have been developed as a resort area on the Caribbean. The one worthy note from a birding interest is that this site is the only place in Nicaragua where Smooth-billed Ani and White-crowned Pigeon can be found.

The Indio Maiz Biological Reserve
San Juan de Nicaragua

Site Description:

Located on the Carribean side of the Indio Maiz Reserve, San Juan de Nicaragua (formerally known as San Juan del Norte) provides access from the east. This side of the reserve is less explored than the forest at Bartola. The reserve encompasses 3,618 km² between the Indio and Maiz rivers and protects a vast area of tropical rainforest. The major part of this area does not allow hiking or other access, as the Ministry of Natural Resources (MARENA) does not allow people to enter the reserve at most places.

San Juan de Nicaragua is on the Indio River, which leads directly into the reserve. Recently, MARENA has begun to allow tourists to enter the reserve using this river, which provides an opportunity to visit this unexplored, remote side of the reserve. This can be done as a day trip to hike the trails and return to San Juan or stay overnight in the reserve.

The native Rama Indians are available as guides at this site. They can guide visitors on the trails or provide a place to stay for an overnight visit. Small settlements of wooden huts are situated along the shores of the Indio River and it may be possible to stay in one of the huts with the Indians for a rustic experience.

Another interesting site located here is the Manatee Lagoon. It will require some time and effort to travel the small creeks that connect the Indio River and this particular lagoon, but it is one of the few places where manatees can be seen in Nicaragua.

Trips to the Indio Maiz Reserve can be arranged in the town of San Juan de Nicaragua. Here it is possible to hire one of the Rama Indians as a guide. The hotels can assist in arranging a variety of trips. This is a rainforest, so bring good hiking boots and a raincoat or umbrella.

Directions:

Travel to San Juan de Nicaragua is available by air from Managua or by boat from San Carlos. Arrangements for transportation can be made with some of the hotels and lodges in the area.

Access/accommodations:

Plush lodging is available at the Rio Indio Lodge, which was established largely for fishing excursions, but the lodge also caters to birders. This lodge features 27 private cabins, each with a screened-in deck. The standard rate is $168 per person (based on double occupancy), plus tax.

Contact:

Phone: Costa Rica (561) 3744-4337
Email: eric@rioindioresort.com
Web Site: www.therioindiolodge.com

Trails:

Rio Indio Lodge offers 6 km of hiking trails on the grounds of the lodge. There is a series of loop trails ranging in length of a few hundred meters to 1.2 km. The outer trails follow the property line of the reserve with several interior trails that go through plantations, forest edge, and rainforest habitat.

Description of Birding Sites:

Birding can be done right on the grounds of the Rio Indio Lodge along its walkways and decks. To get into the forest, a series of hiking trails have been developed. The other option is to travel by boat up the Indio River. Tours are available from the lodge, or you can hire one of the local guides to take you by boat for a day trip or overnight stay on the Indio River.

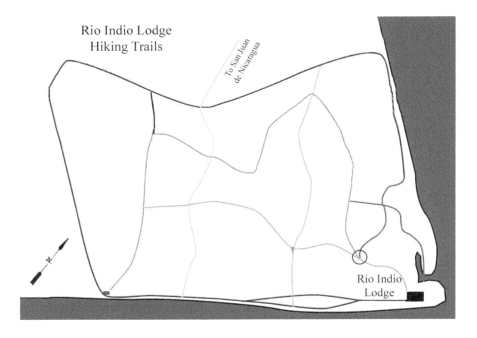

Birds of the Area:

Birds for this portion of the Indio Maiz Reserve are quite similar to the extensive list provided for the Bartola section (p. 127). Below are some of the most sought after species found at this location.

Specialties:

Great Curassow

Agami Heron

King Vulture

Crested Eagle

Rufous-fronted Wood-Quail

Sunbittern

Rufous Nightjar

Crimson-fronted Parakeet

Blue-headed Parrot

Red-lored Parrot

Crested Owl

Rufous-winged Woodpecker

Streak-chested Antpitta

136

Greenfields Private Wildlife Reserve
(*Reserva Silvestre Greenfields*)

Site Description:

Greenfields Wildlife Reserve is a family-owned private reserve founded in 1990 by the Pfranger family. The reserve is located in the Atlantic Lowlands near the village of Kukra Hill, 30 km north of Bluefields. It lies near the Caribbean Coast and encompasses 242 hectares (700 acres) of rainforest, lagoons and wetlands.

The reserve has a series of hiking trails and watercourses for exploring this site by foot or canoe. The mix of lowland forest, wetlands, and open water attract a wide range of bird species.

This reserve offers opportunities for both day visits and over-night stays. The accommodations are nicely done but somewhat expensive. However, it becomes more affordable with more days and larger groups.

Directions:

Greenfields Reserve is located 30 km from the town of Bluefields. From Bluefields it is a 30-minute ride. The dirt road to Kukra Hill was recently completed providing overland travel.

Access/Accommodations:

The lodge offers housing for small groups at a hostel containing six beds. Additional lodging is being developed to upgrade and expand the existing infrastructure. The lodge also has a swimming pool and nearby beach to cool off in during the heat of the day. A day visit to the reserve costs $15 per person. Overnight stays run $140 per couple.

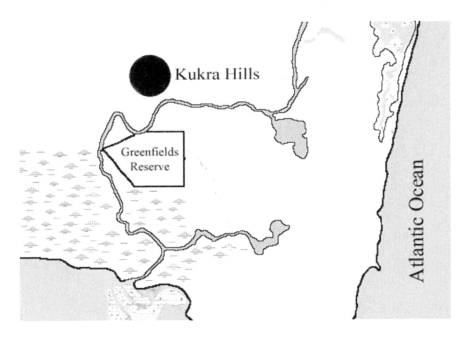

Contact:

Phone: 2268-1897
Email: infogreenfields@ibw.com.ni
Web: www.greenfields.com.ni_

Trails:

Greenfields boasts of having some 30 km (18 miles) of roads, hiking trails and waterways. It can be extensively covered on foot or by canoe that allows access to numerous sections of the reserve.

Description of Birding Sites:

This reserve is best explored and birded by canoe or hiking the numerous trails. Because of the many routes, it is adviseable to go with a guide who can lead you through the reserve.

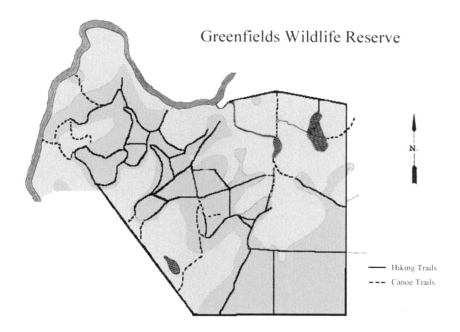

The following bird list is from limited surveys conducted here. This is a rather abbreviated list, and there certainly are many more species to be found at Greenfields.

Rufescent Tiger-Heron

Birds of Greenfields Reserve

Muscovy Duck
Gray-headed Chachalaca
Wood Stork
Neotropic Cormorant
Anhinga
Bare-throated Tiger-Heron
Great Egret
Little Blue Heron
Tricolored Heron
Cattle Egret
Green Heron
Yellow-crowned Night-Heron
Hook-billed Kite
Common Black-Hawk
Great Black-Hawk
Roadside Hawk
Gray-necked Wood-Rail
Northern Jacana
Pale-vented Pigeon
Red-billed Pigeon
Short-billed Pigeon
Blue Ground-Dove
Squirrel Cuckoo
Groove-billed Ani
Collared Aracari
Black-mandibled Toucan
Keel-billed Toucan
Common Pauraque
Green-breasted Mango
Rufous-tailed Hummingbird
Cinnamon Hummingbird
Black-headed Trogon
Ringed Kingfisher
Amazon Kingfisher
Green Kingfisher
White-necked Puffbird
Lineated Woodpecker
Crested Caracara
Laughing Falcon
Olive-throated Parakeet

Orange-chinned Parakeet
White-fronted Parrot
Red-lored Parrot
Mealy Parrot
Yellow-naped Parrot
Yellow Tyrannulet
Yellow-bellied Elaenia
Acadian Flycatcher
White-throated Flycatcher
Dusky-capped Flycatcher
Great Crested Flycatcher
Brown-crested Flycatcher
Gray-capped Flycatcher
Eastern Kingbird
Fork-tailed Flycatcher
Brown Jay
Gray-breasted Martin
House Wren
Clay-colored Thrush
Gray Catbird
Northern Waterthrush
Black-and-white Warbler
Olive-crowned Yellowthroat
American Redstart
Yellow Warbler
Chestnut-sided Warbler
Gray-headed Tanager
Passerini's Tanager
Golden-hooded Tanager
White-collared Seedeater
Yellow-faced Grassquit
Black-striped Sparrow
Summer Tanager
Red-throated Ant-Tanager
Indigo Bunting
Yellow-tailed Oriole
Baltimore Oriole
Chestnut-headed Oropendola
Montezuma Oropendola
Scrub Euphonia

Specialties:

Great Tinamou	White-bellied Emerald
Great Currosow	Am. Pygmy Kingfisher
Rufescent Tiger-Heron	Crimson-fronted Parakeet
Agami Heron	Tawny-throated Leaftosser
Boat-billed Heron	Ruddy Foliage-gleaner
Green Ibis	Gray Kingbird
King Vulture	White-collared Manakin
Spotted Rail	Red-capped Manakin
Sungrebe	Nightingale Wren
Rufous Nightjar	Blue Dacnis
Lesser Nighthawk	Green Honeycreeper
Band-tailed Barbthroat	Nicaraguan Seed-Finch

Collared Aracari

Pearl Lagoon
(*Laguna de Perlas*)

Site Description:

Pearl Lagoon is both the name of a village and coastal lagoon. It is located in the South Caribbean Autonomous Region, about 80 km north of Bluefields. This is Nicaragua's largest coastal lagoon that formed where the Kurinwas River meets the sea. The lagoon is surrounded by mangrove forests and river deltas with a series of small islands located within the lagoon. The Pearl Cays are a group of about 14 small islands located offshore from the Wawashang Natural Reserve and 35 kilometers from Pearl Lagoon. The Pearl Cays are an important nesting site for the endangered Hawksbill Turtle and host a variety of seabirds.

Along the shores of Pearl Lagoon are 18 small indigenous communities of the Garifuna, Criole, Miskito, and Mestizo people, who make a living primarily from harvesting fish, shrimp and lobster. The town of Pearl Lagoon forms the center of the region and offers a few hotels and restaurants to make it a good base to explore the region.

Directions:

Pearl Lagoon can be either reached by boat from Bluefields or by dirt road from the town of El Rama. Taking a boat from Bluefields is a one hour trip. Several boats depart every morning and charge about $10 per person for a one-way trip. The same boats return to Bluefields and leave in the morning but have no set schedule. Private boats can be hired between Bluefields and Pearl Lagoon, giving greater flexibility at a higher price.

Pearl Lagoon can also be reached overland. A dirt road was completed in 2007 and goes from El Rama to Kukra Hill, and then to the town of Pearl Lagoon. This road is in fair condition and provides the easiest way to get to Pearl Lagoon coming from the mainland. It will require about seven hours travel from Managua to reach Pearl Lagoon.

Public Transportation: Options include an air conditioned bus from the Mayoreo Market in Managua, which leaves in the evening, followed by taking a bus that leaves every afternoon at 3:00 pm from El Rama. This bus returns in the morning at 6:00 am, and takes about three hours to complete the route from El Rama to Pearl Lagoon.

From Pearl Lagoon, most sites can only be reached by boat. Private boats offer transportation to places like the Cays (one-hour ride) and also to the many nearby rivers and surrounding villages. Some of these sites are as much as a few hours by boat from the town of Pearl Lagoon. The village of Awas can be reached in about 30 minutes along a trail. There are also small vans that function as buses between Pearl Lagoon and the village of Awas.

Accommodations/Access:

The town of Pearl Lagoon has a few choices of hotels and restaurants for an overnight stay. There is one hotel in the village of Orninoco, where they also provide boat tours of the Wawashang River.

Awas is a very small town close to Pearl Lagoon, established recently by Miskito people. The town is also located on the shores of the lagoon and provides easy access to the lagoon. It is known for its swimming beach but also provides access to a palm savanna habitat. Several small creeks traverse the open plain. Hiking and canoeing are offered in Awas.

Description of Birding Sites:

Birding can be conducted by boat, kayak, or canoe along the lagoon and the numerous rivers. Boats can also be hired for a trip to the Pearl Islands for birds of the coast and open water habitat. Walking on the trail from Pearl Lagoon to Awas and other local dirt roads offer opportunities for forest and forest edge species.

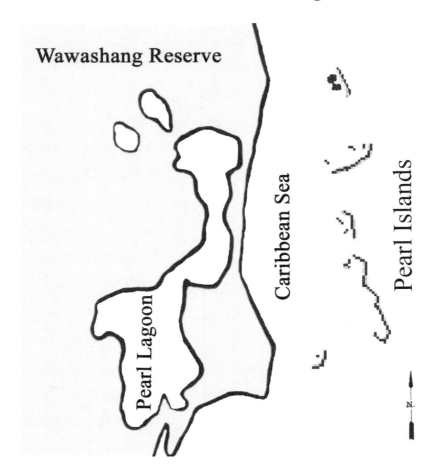

Common Birds of the Area:

This area contains a wide variety of birds of the rainforest and forest edge in the forest surrounding the lagoon, plus birds of the open land around the villages. The lagoon provides habitat for a range of wetland and open water birds, and a trip to the Pearl Islands will provide the possibility of observing a variety of sea birds, a group of birds that remains poorly studied.

Additional Sites

Corn Islands

The Corn Islands consist of two larger islands off the northeast coast of Nicaragua. There islands have largely been developed as a tourist destination, and as a result are easy to reach. The best birding at this site is the opportunity to see a variety of seabirds. This is also the only known site in Nicaragua to find Smooth-billed Ani and White-crowned Pigeon. While the Groove-billed Ani is very common throughout the country, Smooth-billed Ani has a very limited distribution in Central America. The White-crowned Pigeon is found primarily on the larger islands in the Caribbean and is also of limited occurrence in Central America.

Corn Islands

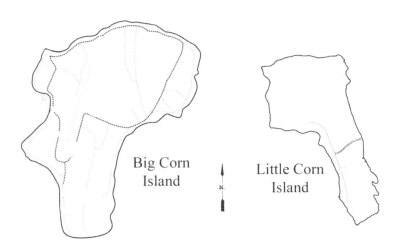

Big Corn Island

Little Corn Island

The map indicates the main roads on these two small islands, shown separately. Travel to Big Corn Island is available by air travel, while all other local travel in the area is by boat.

Bosawas Biosphere Reserve
(*Reserva de la Biosfera Bosawás*)

The Bosawas Biosphere Reserve in northern Nicaragua is an area of rolling hills and tropical forest. In 1997, this reserve was designated as a UNESCO Biosphere Reserve. This is the largest reserve in Central America and encompasses approximately 2 million hectares (4,940,000 acres) of land or about 15% of Nicaragua's land area.

The name Bosawas comes from the combined names of three natural features; the Bocay River, Mount Saslaya and the Waspuk River. The Isabella Mountains form the highlands on the western side of the reserve with numerous rivers draining to the lowlands to the east. The Coco River and the border with Honduras form the northern boundary.

Bosawas Reserve lies within the homelands of two of Nicaragua's indigenous peoples, the Sumos and the Miskito. Like most of Nicaragua's reserve, people live within its boundaries with some 130,000 inhabitants relying on subsistence farming. Due to uncontrolled encroachment, Bosawas is threated by illegal logging, slash-and-burn farming and other human activities that have fragmented this area. However, this enormous area is still quite unexplored and rich in its wildlife and forest land.

For those wishing to visit the Bosawas Reserve, permission must first be obtained from the Ministry of Environment and Natural Resources (MARENA) before entering. Contact the ministry office at:

> Reserva de la Biosfera Bosawas
> Apartado Postal 5123, Managua
> Phone: 2233-1594

They will also provide information about necessary vaccinations in this region and travel information. The Nicaraguan government also requires tourists to hire a guide to explore this reserve. Guides can be arranged in the community of El Hormiguero.

Most travelers enter Bosawas through the town of Siuna. There is bus service from Managua, which takes about nine hours and costs about $5 each way. Another option is to fly on La Costena airlines. The cost for a round trip ticket is $42.50 per person.

Accommodations are available around Siuna, but many of these are quite primitive with some lacking running water. Therefore, it is important to be prepared for a trip to this region and to have proper gear for various weather conditions. Also, be sure to travel with an experienced guide.

There are also options to explore the region along some of the rivers, such as the Coco and Bocay Rivers. Boats depart from the town of Wiwili, which is a five hour bus ride from Jinotega, or from Ayapal, which is about nine to ten hours from Jinogeta. To go up the river to Raiti and back takes about a week. There are no accommodations along the way, so bring your own tent to camp along the riverbank at night. Wiwili has four hotels that can help arrange boat rental. You will need to provide your own food, water, and camping equipment. Traveling in this region is quite demanding!

Saslaya National Park
(*Parque Nacional Cerro Saslaya*)

Saslaya National Park lies within the Bosawas Reserve, but has been designated as a national park. This park is also very remote, but it protects the forests covering the Saslaya peak. This site has been surveyed for its bird life, but much remains to be discovered here. There is no complete list of birds for this area and for those adventurous birders willing to travel here, there exists an opportunity to add to our understanding of the occurrence and distribution of a number of species in Nicaragua.

Northern Highlands

Three-wattled Bellbird

Region 5
Northern Highlands;
Oak-Pine Forests and Cloud Forests

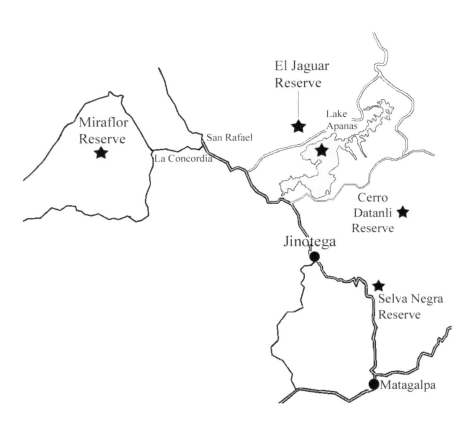

Northern Highlands Jinotega/ Matagalpa Area

The Northern Highlands are the most mountainous part of Nicaragua and the road between Matagalpa and Jinotega is among the most scenic roads in the country. This is an area of coffee plantations surrounded by pastures, with tropical pine forests on the drier slopes and cloud forest remnants on the upper reaches of the highest peaks.

The Northern Highlands mark the southern-most extent of the oak-pine forest, which stretches south from Mexico through northern Central America. As a result, there are several species of birds that reach the southern extent of their range in this part of Nicaragua.

Several protected areas have been established in this region, including Cerro Datanli-El Diablo, Volcan Yali, and Miraflor Reserve. There are also several private reserves and lodges that offer accommodations and great birding opportunities, including Selva Negra Reserve, La Bastilla Ecolodge and El Jaguar Reserve. These reserves are coffee farms with protected cloud forest remnants. Over 300 bird species have been recorded here, including the Resplendent Quetzal.

Located within a broad valley between two mountain ranges lies Lake Apanas, the largest artificial lake in Nicaragua. This lake is a short drive from Jinotega, and a dirt road has been built which goes around it. With a mix of cloud forests, oak-pine forests, and Lake Apanas, this is a very diverse section of the country that provides an opportunity to see a large variety of birds.

The city of Jinotega is located close to several reserves and has a range of restaurants and hotels to provide a base from which to explore this region. While much of Nicaragua is low-lying with a hot-humid climate, this region is much cooler with temperatures usually between 65 and 75 degrees. The highest elevations can actually become quite cold at night.

Moyua Lagoon and Wetland
(*Laguna de Moyuá*)

Site Description:

This site is somewhat similar to Tisma Lagoon, but is included in this section as it is an easy stop along the way to the Northern Highlands from the Managua/Granada area.

Moyua Lagoon is an area of extensive shallow water and emergant vegetation located along the Managua-Matagalpa Highway and recently designated Ramsar site. The area adjacent to the highway is easy to observe from the edge of the road, particularly during periods of high water when open water provides an unobstructed view of the lagoon. During times of drought, the water area can be significantly reduced, and the emergent plants can make it difficult to search for birds of open water habitat.

Directions:

The Managua-Matagalpa Highway runs along a portion of the eastern edge of the Moyua Lagoon. At Km 69 a turn-out is located on the west side of the road (left side when heading north). Be careful of sudden drop-offs between the pavement and gravel shoulder of the road.

Access:

It may be possible to access the wetland by boat during highwater or walking among the vegetation, which can be challenging. However, birds of the open water and wetland habitats are not much different than what can be found at Tisma Lagoon or other nearby sites. This area mostly provides an area for a quick stop along the way for water birds that can be difficult to find in other areas due to the lack of wetlands.

Birds of Moyua Lagoon and Wetland

Blue-winged Teal can be abundant here, plus a variety of herons, egrets, Common Gallinule, American Coot and Northern Jacana.

Northern Jacana

Selva Negra Reserve
(*Reserva Silvestre Privada Selva Negra*)

Site Description:

Selva Negra is a coffee plantation with montane and cloud forest located on the upper slopes beyond the resort and plantation. This site is well known for its cool weather and German-style food and lodging. The Selva Negra (Black Forest) Mountain Resort has been developed with numerous cabins and is a popular place for people to dine, hike in the forest, or take advantage of the accommodations for a variety of occasions. The site includes three conference centers with a capacity for more than 500 people, so check ahead to avoid crowds during special event. If you come during the week it is usually quiet and provides quaint accommodations and good birding in the forest. There is also a rustic stone chapel that is popular for weddings of Managua's well-to-do.

Selva Negra is a coffee farm based on the German tradition of chalets set around a peaceful pond with access to hiking trails up the adjoining 200 hectare (500 acre) hillside forest and along its ridge. The farm was purchased by the current owners in 1975 and totals 610 hectares (1,500 acres). It is roughly divided equally into one-third forest, one-third coffee plantation, and one-third pasture, roads, and housing.

The area is a birder's destination with some 250 species of birds recorded here, including the range-restricted Bushy-crested Jay. Tours of the coffee farm and forest are available and conducted in Spanish, English, and German when Mausi Kuhl is available. The Selva Negra restaurant includes a family museum with historical pictures and relicts from the 19th century when a number of German farmers came to the region to become coffee growers.

Directions:

Selva Negra is located about 2 hours north of Managua. Travel north through Tipitapa and continue to Matagalpa going past the Jinotega exit.

Selva Negra is located on the Matagalpa-Jinotega Highway at Km 139.5. The entrance to Selva Negra is marked by an old military tank on the side of the road, a relic from the revolution. This coffee plantation and preserve are easily reached without four-wheel drive.

Access/Accommodations:

The entrance road goes through the coffee plantation for 1.5 km before reaching the restaurant and resort. Rooms run from $15 for a bed in the youth hostel to $45 for a double overlooking the lake or $85 for a private bungalow.

Entrance to the resort is about $5 for day visits, which can be applied toward a meal, and provides access to the hiking trails. The restaurant offers an excellent menu of fine German cooking and traditional Nicaraguan meals. Prices range from about $5 to $20 for breakfasts, lunch, and full dinners.

Contact Information:

Phone: 2772-3883/5713
Email: reservaciones@selvanegra.ni
Website: www.selvanegra.com

You can also arrange tours from their daughter's US coffeehouse in Atlanta, Georgia: wwwjavavino.com.

Trails:

The reserve includes a series of 14 hiking trails that lead throughout the forest. The trails range in difficulty and length, but all lead through the montane or dense cloud forest that is home to over 250 species of birds.

If you take one of the tougher, steeper hikes, you will be rewarded with some splendid views of the city of Matagalpa and the mountains surrounding it.

Description of Birding Sites:

Walking around the grounds by the cabins and along the entrance road can be productive for parrots, motmots, Brown Jay, thrushes and other species. This is a good place to find Bushy-crested Jay. While the forest is the primary focus of this property, birding around the coffee plantation and pasture can produce a different variety of birds. Recent additions to the reserve bird list have come from the pasture, as this had been a poorly surveyed area.

The trails into the forest are the highlight of this reserve and provide access to different forest types in the lower and higher elevations. Trails along the lower slopes provide easier walking with steeper trails on the upper slopes where the cloud forest is found.

In winter, Wood Thrush and a variety of migrant warblers can be found here among the resident species. The Three-wattled Bellbird can be easily heard on mountainous trails during the breeding season (March to September). Scaled Ant-pittas feed along the trails at dusk, and Resplendent Quetzal has also been sighted here.

Selva Negra Reserve

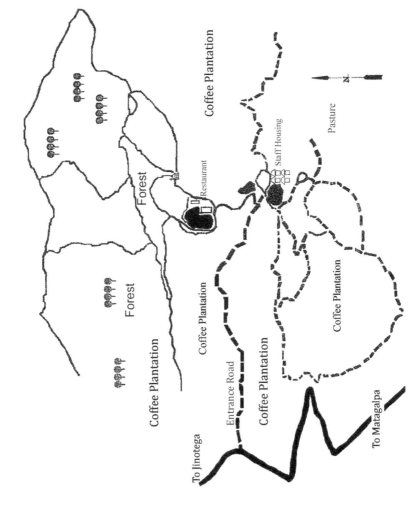

Birds of Selva Negra Reserve

Great Tinamou
Little Tinamou
Crested Bobwhite
Swallow-tailed Kite
Double-toothed Kite
Plumbeous Kite
Mississippi Kite
Sharp-shinned Hawk
Gray Hawk
Short-tailed Hawk
Red-billed Pigeon
Blue Ground-Dove
Black-billed Cuckoo
Striped Owl
Black-and-white Owl
Ferruginous Pygmy-Owl
Mottled Owl
Great Swallow-tailed Swift
Long-billed Hermit
Little Hermit
Green Violetear
Violet-headed Hummingbird
Fork-tailed Emerald
Violet-crowned Woodnymph
Azure-crowned Hummingbird
Blue-tailed Hummingbird
Stripe-tailed Hummingbird
Scaly-breasted Hummingbird
Blue-crowned Motmot
Turquoise-browed Motmot
Gartered Trogon
Collared Trogon
Emerald Toucanet
Collared Aracari
Keel-billed Toucan
Smoky-brown Woodpecker
Golden-olive Woodpecker
Black-cheeked Woodpecker
Laughing Falcon
Bat Falcon

Green Parakeet
Orange-chinned Parakeet
Orange-fronted Parakeet
Brown-hooded Parrot
White-crowned Parrot
White-fronted Parrot
Barred Antshrike
Plain Antvireo
Slaty Antwren
Dusky Antbird
Buff-throated Foliage-gleaner
Ruddy Woodcreeper
Strong-billed Woodcreeper
No. Barred Woodcreeper
Ivory-billed Woodcreeper
Spotted Woodcreeper
Spot-crowned Woodcreeper
Yellow-bellied Elaenia
Mountain Elaenia
Ochre-bellied Flycatcher
Sepia-capped Flycatcher
Eye-ringed Flatbill
Yellow-olive Flycatcher
Streaked Flycatcher
Tufted Flycatcher
Olive-sided Flycatcher
Eastern Wood-Pewee
Tropical Pewee
Yellow-bellied Flycatcher
Willow Flycatcher
White-throated Flycatcher
Yellowish Flycatcher
Bright-rumped Attila
Rufous Mourner
Dusky-capped Flycatcher
Gray-capped Flycatcher
Sulphur-bellied Flycatcher
Piratic Flycatcher
Western Kingbird
Rufous Piha

Black-and-white Becard
Rose-throated Becard
Masked Tityra
Yellow-throated Vireo
Blue-headed Vireo
Philadelphia Vireo
Red-eyed Vireo
Lesser Greenlet
Brown Jay
Rufous-and-white Wren
Rufous-browed Wren
White-breasted Wood-Wren
Gray-breasted Wood-Wren
Spot-breasted Wren
White-lored Gnatcatcher
Veery
Swainson's Thrush
Wood Thrush
Mountain Thrush
White-throated Thrush
Gray Catbird
Cedar Waxwing
Ovenbird
Worm-eating Warbler
Louisiana Waterthrush
Northern Waterthrush
Prothonotary Warbler
Crescent-chested Warbler
MacGillivray's Warbler
Kentucky Warbler

Olive-crowned Yellowthroat
Gray-crowned Yellowthroat
Hooded Warbler
American Redstart
Cape May Warbler
Cerulean Warbler
Tropical Parula
Bay-breasted Warbler
Blackburnian Warbler
Yellow-throated Warbler
Townsend's Warbler
Hermit Warbler
Fan-tailed Warbler
Golden-crowned Warbler
Canada Warbler
Wilson's Warbler
Gray-headed Tanager
Crimson-collared Tanager
Golden-hooded Tanager
Rufous-winged Tanager
Chestnut-capped Brush-Finch
White-naped Brush-Finch
Common Bush-Tanager
Hepatic Tanager
Summer Tanager
Scarlet Tanager
White-winged Tanager
Red-crowned Ant-Tanager
Red-throated Ant-Tanager
Blue Seedeater
Scrub Euphonia

In addition to the forest, the man-made pond attracts a variety of birds.

Black-bellied Whistling-Duck
Great Blue Heron
Little Blue Heron
Great Egret
Green Heron
Least Grebe
Pied-billed Grebe
Northern Jacana

Common Gallinule
American Coot
Purple Gallinule
White-throated Crake
Solitary Sandpiper
Spotted Sandpiper
Amazon Kingfisher
Green Kingfisher

Specialties:

Thicket Tinamou
Slaty-breasted Tinamou
Highland Guan
Great Curassow
White-faced Quail-Dove
Striped Cuckoo
Pheasant Cuckoo
Lesser Ground-Cuckoo
Green-breasted Mountain-gem
Sparkling-tailed Hummingbird
Emerald-chinned Hummingbird
Black-crested Coquette
White-eared Hummingbird
Resplendent Quetzal
Barred Forest-Falcon
Collared Forest-Falcon
Barred Parakeet
Black-faced Antthrush

Scaled Antpitta
Fulvous-bellied Antpitta
Northern Bentbill
Golden-crowned Spadebill
Stub-tailed Spadebill
Northern Shiffornis
Three-wattled Bellbird
Long-billed Gnatwren
White-ruffed Manakin
Tawny-crowned Greenlet
Rufous-browed Peppershrike
Nightingale Wren
Slate-colored Solitaire
Orange-billed Nightingale-Thrush
Black-hd. Nightingale-Thrush
Bushy-crested Jay
Golden-winged Warbler
Yellow-winged Tanager

Bushy-crested Jay

Cerro Datanli - El Diablo Reserve
(*Reserva Natural Cerro Datanlí-El Diablo*)

La Bastilla Lodge and surrounding forest.

Site Description:

The Cerro Datanli-El Diablo Reserve is located in the highlands of north-central Nicaragua. The reserve was established in 1991 and is comprised of 5,848 hectares (14,450 acres). It ranges in elevation from 700 meters to 1,680 meters (2,296 to 5,512 feet) at El Diablo Peak.

The reserve is a mosaic of private lands with some 300 landowners holding title under agreements to manage the land for conservation purposes. The area is a mix of coffee plantations with oak-pine forest and cloud forest. To date, 205 species of birds have been recorded here.

The reserve is located in the Dariense mountain range, northeast of Jinotega. The reserve can be accessed from various directions by several dirt roads leading to the few small villages located there. This reserve was established to protect the mountain forest that is being threatened by deforestation for timber extraction and encroaching agriculture.

Directions:

The area where the reserve is located has both public and private access roads that allow vehicles to enter from different sides of the reserve. From the Matagalpa-Jinotega Highway, turn off at the La Fundadora junction. The area roads lead to the villages La Fundadora, Esmeralda and La Parranda, which allow entrance to the reserve from the south, east, or west sides. To find La Bastilla, see next section.

Directions to La Bastille:

The La Bastilla Ecolodge is located within the Datanli-El Diablo Reserve, 27 kilometers from Jinotega at an elevation of 1,200 meters. Turn off of the Jinotega Highway about 3 km north of the city at Km 165. Turn right onto the paved road just before the river. Follow the road for 12 km along the east shore of Lake Apanas.

After 9 km the pavement ends. At the second road after a river crossing, turn right and follow a dirt road for about 9.5 km to reach the ecolodge. A sign marks the turn-off from the main road. At the lodge, park at the bottom and walk up as the road is very steep, even for four-wheel drive.

La Bastilla Ecolodge
Cerro Datanli Reserve

Lake Apanas

La Bastilla

Jinotega

Access/Accommodations:

This ecolodge is managed by students involved in a local educational project supervised by professionals. Therefore, funds from the hotel help support an education program in this rural area.

The lodge offers comfortable rooms and a continental breakfast, and there is also an option to camp on a wooden deck. Tents, foldable beds, bedding, towels and even a private bath with solar-powered hot water are provided.

Rooms begin at $60 per night for a double. Dormatory rooms are $15 per person per night with a capacity for 30 people and camping is $10 per night. The restaurant is open from 6:00 am to 9:00 pm with meals averaging $3 to $9. An entrance fee of $5 is charged for day use and includes coffee.

La Bastilla Ecolodge Contact Information:

Phone: 2782-4335 (Jinotega office)
            8654-6235 (cell phone at the lodge)
Email: reservaciones@bastillaecolodge.com
Website: www.bastillaecolodge.com

Trails:

A series of hiking trails lead through the reserve. There are two trails from La Bastilla, including a 7 km hike to El Gobiado (about a 2 hour walk). There also is a trail leading from La Esmeralda to La Trampa that can be approached from either side.

Description of Birding Sites:

Birding can be done along any of the dirt roads that lead through the reserve or along any of the hiking trails. Check for maps and directions at La Bastilla or any of the other small villages where the trails begin.

Cerro Datanli Trail Map

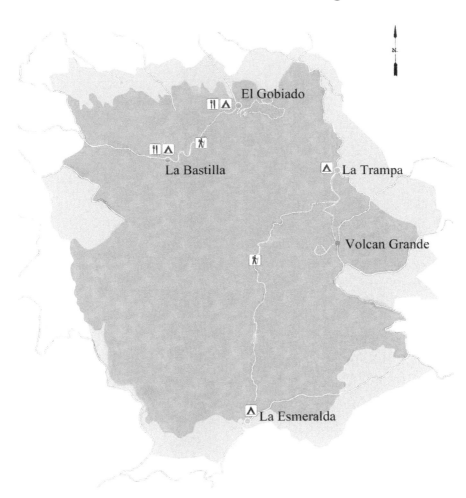

Birds of Cerro Datanli

Great Tinamou
Plain Chachalaca
Gray-headed Chachalaca
Crested Bobwhite
Green Heron
Hook-billed Kite
Swallow-tailed Kite
White-tailed Kite
Great Black-Hawk
Harris's Hawk
Roadside Hawk
Swainson's Hawk
Red-tailed Hawk
Black Hawk-Eagle
Red-billed Pigeon
Band-tailed Pigeon
Gray-headed Dove
White-faced Quail-Dove
Ferruginous Pygmy-Owl
Mottled Owl
Common Potoo
Northern Potoo
Long-billed Hermit
Stripe-throated Hermit
Violet Sabrewing
Canivet's Emerald
Violet-crowned Woodnymph
White-bellied Emerald
Azure-crowned Hummingbird
Rufous-tailed Hummingbird
Cinnamon Hummingbird
Stripe-tailed Hummingbird
Ruby-throated Hummingbird
Black-headed Trogon
Gartered Trogon
Elegant Trogon
Collared Trogon
Blue-crowned Motmot
Keel-billed Motmot
Turquoise-browed Motmot

Emerald Toucanet
Collared Aracari
Keel-billed Toucan
Acorn Woodpecker
Smoky-brown Woodpecker
Golden-olive Woodpecker
Lineated Woodpecker
Pale-billed Woodpecker
Barred Forest-Falcon
Crested Caracara
American Kestrel
Bat Falcon
Orange-fronted Parakeet
Orange-chinned Parakeet
Brown-hooded Parrot
White-crowned Parrot
White-fronted Parrot
Barred Antshrike
Russet Antshrike
Slaty Antwren
Black-faced Antthrush
Olivaceous Woodcreeper
Plain-brown Woodcreeper
Ruddy Woodcreeper
Northern Barred Woodcreeper
Strong-billed Woodcreeper
Spotted Woodcreeper
Streaked-headed Woodcreeper
Buff-throated Foliage-gleaner
Mountain Elaenia
Ochre-bellied Flycatcher
Sepia-capped Flycatcher
Common Tody-Flycatcher
Eye-ringed Flatbill
Yellow-olive Flycatcher
Royal Flycatcher
Western Wood-Pewee
Olive-sided Flycatcher
Eastern Wood-Pewee
Tropical Pewee

Yellow-bellied Flycatcher
Least Flycatcher
Yellowish Flycatcher
Black Phoebe
Bright-rumped Attila
Dusky-capped Flycatcher
Ash-throated Flycatcher
Great Crested Flycatcher
Boat-billed Flycatcher
Streaked Flycatcher
Sulphur-bellied Flycatcher
Western Kingbird
White-ruffed Manakin
Red-capped Manakin
Black-crowned Tityra
Masked Tityra
Gray-collared Becard
Yellow-throated Vireo
Blue-headed Vireo
Red-eyed Vireo
Yellow-green Vireo
Tawny-crowned Greenlet
Lesser Greenlet
Rufous-browed Peppershrike
White-throated Magpie-Jay
Brown Jay
Bushy-crested Jay
Band-backed Wren
Rufous-naped Wren
Spot-breasted Wren
Rufous-and-white Wren
Plain Wren
White-breasted Wood-Wren
Gray-breasted Wood-Wren
Orange-billed Nightingale-Thrush
Black-headed Nightingale-Thrush
Swainson's Thrush
Wood Thrush
Clay-colored Thrush
Ovenbird
Louisiana Waterthrush
Northern Waterthrush

Black-and-white Warbler
Tennessee Warbler
Kentucky Warbler
Common Yellowthroat
Northern Parula
Tropical Parula
Blackburnian Warbler
Yellow Warbler
Chestnut-sided Warbler
Yellow-throated Warbler
Black-throated Green Warbler
Rufous-capped Warbler
Golden-crowned Warbler
Canada Warbler
Wilson's Warbler
Gray-headed Tanager
Crimson-collared Tanager
Passerini's Tanager
Rufous-winged Tanager
Thick-billed Seed-Finch
Grayish Saltator
Buff-throated Saltator
Black-headed Saltator
Black-striped Sparrow
White-naped Brush-Finch
Common Bush Tanager
Scarlet Tanager
Western Tanager
White-winged Tanager
Red-crowned Ant-Tanager
Red-throated Ant-Tanager
Rose-breasted Grosbeak
Blue Bunting
Orchard Oriole
Yellow-backed Oriole
Yellow-tailed Oriole
Altamira Oriole
Montezuma Oropendola
Scrub Euphonia
Yellow-throated Euphonia
Elegant Euphonia
Blue-crowned Chlorophonia

Specialties:

Highland Guan
Black-eared Wood-Quail
Spotted Wood-Quail
Violaceous Quail-Dove
Ruddy Quail-Dove
Pheasant Cuckoo
White-eared Hummingbird
Green-breasted Mountain-gem
Resplendent Quetzal
White-flanked Antshrike

Tawny-winged Woodcreeper
Three-wattled Bellbird
Nightingale Wren
Slate-colored Solitaire
Golden-winged Warbler
Golden-cheeked Warbler
Townsend's Warbler
Yellow-winged Tanager
Golden-hooded Tanager
White-eared Ground-Sparrow
Chestnut-headed Oropendola

Resplendant Quetzal

EL Jaguar Reserve
(*Reserva Silvestre Privada El Jaguar*)

Site Description:

The El Jaguar Reserve is a birder-owned reserve and coffee farm. It is located about 4 hours north of Managua atop the Isabelia Mountain Range. The reserve is located at 1,350 m (4430 ft) above sea level in a cloud forest. The annual rainfall is 80 inches, and the temperature varies from 46°F to 90°F (8°C to 32°C).

The reserve is run by Georges and Lillie Duriaux-Chavarria who operate the reserve and coffee plantation. The farm has been in family hands for more than 50 years. Their stated goal is to protect the biodiversity of the cloud forest and to produce high quality, environmentally-friendly coffee in harmony with nature. Their vision for the reserve is to be a model of sustainable production with its components of environment protection, organic production, and social sustainability.

Of the 199 acres that comprise this farm, 70 acres are a preserved forest, and 60 more are managed woods for a total of 130 acres of cloud forest. Interwoven among this are 13 coffee parcels totaling 34 acres. The other 35 acres are grassland that have been set aside for potential coffee production without further impacting the surrounding forest.

The cloud forest has a subtropical climate with high humity, most of it derived from low clouds or fog that envelops the forest. The forest is comprised of giant oak and fern trees that support a high diversity of plants and animals. To date, nearly 300 species of birds have been recorded in this reserve, and birders have sighted over 50 species of birds on the trails of El Jaguar in a single day.

In 2002, a research team participating in the National Important Bird Areas Program rediscovered the Golden-cheeked Warbler at El Jaguar for the first time in Nicaragua since 1891. Among other discoveries the team found 4 new species for Nicaragua, and in just three days they recorded 106 species at El Jaguar Reserve. This reserve is also a Christmas Bird Count site and conducts bird population monitoring at established bird banding sites on the property.

Directions:

El Jaguar is located 188 kilometers from Managua. From Jinotega, drive north 14 km toward San Juan del Norte. At Km 175.7 turn onto a dirt road where you will see a sign for El Jaguar. Continue 4.9 km to Sisle, going through Sasle, a small village with a similar name. Turn left at the bus stop.

Follow this road 3 km to the turnoff indicated by a sign for Finca El Jaguar. Turn left and go another 1.1 km to the entrance. It is another 0.5 km down the entrance road to reach the office. A four-wheel drive vehicle is required to reach the reserve.

El Jaguar Reserve

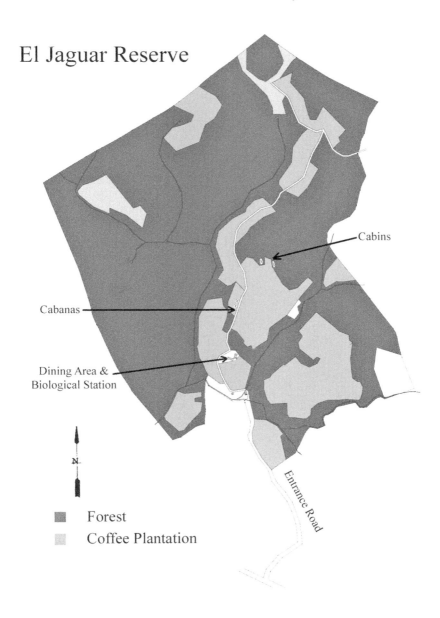

Cabins

Cabanas

Dining Area &
Biological Station

N

Forest
Coffee Plantation

Entrance Road

Access/Accommodations:

This reserve offers several trails and great bird watching possibilities, as well as cabins for tourists and a biological station for students or biologists.

The reserve has a small lodge with two apartments, including one with 2 rooms and the other with 3 rooms. Total capacity is nine people. Each apartment has a shared toilet and shower, and an equipped kitchenette. Food and drinks are available at the reserve.

They have also recently constructed two cabanas, each with two twin beds and glass doors that open to a deck overlooking the coffee plantation and forested slope. Cost is $70 per night.

Biological Station: A biological station has been constructed to lodge professionals and students. It contains three rooms with bunk beds for 20 people and conference area for meeting and seminars for 40 people.

They accept reservations for a minimum of two nights and ask that you book at least three days in advance.

Contact Information:

Reserva Nebliselva El Jaguar
Phone: 505-2279-9219 505 279 9219 • 88 61 016
Email: georges.duriaux@gmail.com
Website: www.jaguarreserve.org

Trails:

There are 4 different trails to walk through the reserve, varying in length from 1 km to 2.6 km. Trails are easy to moderately difficult, however due to the high rainfall and clay soil, the trails are often quite muddy and slippery following rain, making walking a bit challenging, so be prepared for this. The trails have been developed and maintained as well as possible considering these factors. For day visitors, the reserve's entrance fee is $10, and this includes a guide.

The various trails are:

El Jurásico	1 km	
Golden-winged Warbler	2.6 km	(Interpretive Trail)
El Jaguar	1.8 km	
El Puma	2 km	
Coffee Tours	(1.5 hours)	

El Jaguar Trail Map

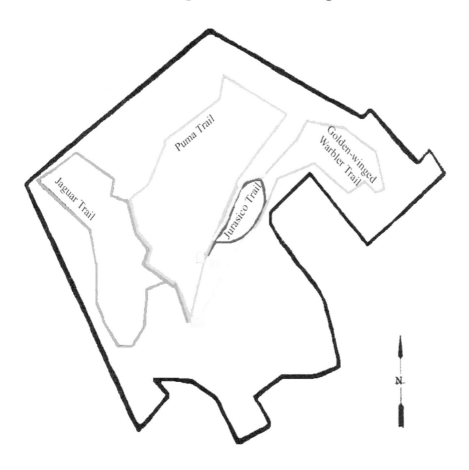

Description of Birding Sites:

The various trails wander through secondary forest, primary cloud forest, forest edge and openings, and among the coffee plantation. With the dense forest cover and rich cloud forest habitat, you can walk these trails several days in a row and continue to discover new birds. Walking can be slow and difficult in the heavy wet clay, and birds may be difficult to see in the dense forest and occasional fog, but the effort will be rewarded with great birding potential. Due to the rain and fog typical of a cloud forest, it is recommended to spend several days here to optimize birding.

Between hikes on the trail system, be sure to spend time at the bird feeding station located by the Biological Station and new dining hall. Bunches of bananas are hung to attract a variety of tanagers and even Tennessee Warblers, and hummingbird feeders attract Violet Saberwing among other species. Verbena shrubs have been planted to lure other species of hummingbirds as well. Sitting here can be very rewarding and provide excellent opportunities for wildlife photographers.

From about October through January, Highland Guans come to feed at the old kitchen site at sunrise, located along the entrance road. This is the best place in the country to see this rare species, which comes out of the forest to feed alongside the chickens.

Specialty Birds:

Thicket Tinamou	Plain Antvireo
Slaty-breasted Tinamou	Three-wattled Bellbird
Highland Guan	Bushy-crested Jay
Great Curassow	Gray-breasted Wood-Wren
Emerald-chinned Hummingbird	Slate-colored Solitaire
White-eared Hummingbird	Black-headed Nightingale-Thrush
Stripe-tailed Hummingbird	Golden-winged Warbler
Green-breasted Mountain-gem	Golden-cheeked Warbler
Azure-crowned Hummingbird	Yellow-winged Tanager
Crested Owl	Golden-hooded Tanager
Northern Pygmy-Owl	Bay-headed Tanager
Tawny-winged Woodcreeper	Rufous-collared Sparrow

Birds of El Jaguar Reserve

Great Tinamou
Little Tinamou
Plain Chachalaca
Gray-headed Chachalaca
Crested Bobwhite
Gray-headed Kite
Hook-billed Kite
Swallow-tailed Kite
Plumbeous Kite
Sharp-shinned Hawk
Semiplumbeous Hawk
Common Black-Hawk
Gray Hawk
White-tailed Hawk
Black Hawk-Eagle
Red-billed Pigeon
Blue Ground-Dove
Gray-headed Dove
Gray-chested Dove
White-faced Quail-Dove
Violaceous Quail-Dove
Ruddy Quail-Dove
Yellow-billed Cuckoo
Black-billed Cuckoo
Striped Cuckoo
Pheasant Cuckoo
Lesser Roadrunner
Mottled Owl
Black-and-white Owl
Common Potoo
Northern Potoo
Bronzy Hermit
Long-billed Hermit
Stripe-throated Hermit
Violet Sabrewing
Green Violetear
Canivet's Emerald
Violet-crowned Woodnymph
Blue-throated Goldentail
White-bellied Emerald

Blue-chested Hummingbird
Blue-tailed Hummingbird
Steely-vented Hummingbird
Rufous-tailed Hummingbird
Cinnamon Hummingbird
Plain-capped Starthroat
Sparkling-tailed Hummingbird
Ruby-throated Hummingbird
Black-headed Trogon
Gartered Trogon
Collared Trogon
Blue-crowned Motmot
Rufous-tailed Jacamar
Emerald Toucanet
Collared Aracari
Keel-billed Toucan
Yellow-bellied Sapsucker
Smoky-brown Woodpecker
Golden-olive Woodpecker
Northern Flicker
Lineated Woodpecker
Pale-billed Woodpecker
Barred Forest-Falcon
Collared Forest-Falcon
Laughing Falcon
Bat Falcon
Olive-throated Parakeet
Barred Parakeet
White-crowned Parrot
White-fronted Parrot
Red-lored Parrot
Barred Antshrike
Slaty Antwren
Scaled Antpitta
Black-faced Antthrush
Tawny-throated Leaftosser
Scaly-throated Foliage-gleaner
Buff-throated Foliage-gleaner
Ruddy Foliage-gleaner
Ruddy Woodcreeper

Strong-billed Woodcreeper
Northern Barred Woodcreeper
Spotted Woodcreeper
Spot-crowned Woodcreeper
Greenish Elaenia
Mountain Elaenia
Ochre-bellied Flycatcher
Sepia-capped Flycatcher
Scale-crested Pygmy-Tyrant
Northern Bentbill
Common Tody-Flycatcher
Eye-ringed Flatbill
Yellow-olive Flycatcher
Stub-tailed Spadebill
Olive-sided Flycatcher
Eastern Wood-Pewee
Tropical Pewee
Yellow-bellied Flycatcher
Acadian Flycatcher
Alder Flycatcher
Least Flycatcher
Yellowish Flycatcher
Bright-rumped Attila
Dusky-capped Flycatcher
Nutting's Flycatcher
Boat-billed Flycatcher
Gray-capped Flycatcher
Sulphur-bellied Flycatcher
Piratic Flycatcher
Western Kingbird
White-ruffed Manakin
Red-capped Manakin
Masked Tityra
Northern Shiffornis
Speckled Mourner
White-winged Becard
Gray-collared Becard
Rose-throated Becard
Yellow-throated Vireo
Blue-headed Vireo
Philadelphia Vireo
Red-eyed Vireo

Yellow-green Vireo
Tawny-crowned Greenlet
Lesser Greenlet
Rufous-browed Peppershrike
Brown Jay
Band-backed Wren
Spot-breasted Wren
Rufous-and-white Wren
Plain Wren
White-breasted Wood-Wren
Gray-breasted Wood-Wren
Orange-billed Nightingale-Thrush
Veery
Gray-cheeked Thrush
Swainson's Thrush
Wood Thrush
Cedar Waxwing
Ovenbird
Worm-eating Warbler
Louisiana Waterthrush
Northern Waterthrush
Blue-winged Warbler
Black-and-white Warbler
Prothonotary Warbler
Tennessee Warbler
MacGillivray's Warbler
Mourning Warbler
Kentucky Warbler
Gray-crowned Yellowthroat
Hooded Warbler
American Redstart
Cerulean Warbler
Northern Parula
Tropical Parula
Magnolia Warbler
Bay-breasted Warbler
Blackburnian Warbler
Yellow Warbler
Chestnut-sided Warbler
Townsend's Warbler
Black-throated Green Warbler
Black-throated Blue Warbler

Fan-tailed Warbler
Rufous-capped Warbler
Golden-crowned Warbler
Buff-rumped Warbler
Canada Warbler
Wilson's Warbler
Yellow-breasted Chat
Crimson-collared Tanager
Passerini's Tanager
Rufous-winged Tanager
Shining Honeycreeper
Red-legged Honeycreeper
Green Honeycreeper
Thick-billed Seed-Finch
Yellow-faced Grassquit
Grayish Saltator
Buff-throated Saltator
Black-headed Saltator
Chestnut-capped Brush-Finch
Olive Sparrow
Black-striped Sparrow
White-naped Brush-Finch
Rusty Sparrow
Stripe-headed Sparrow
Chipping Sparrow

Rufous-collared Sparrow
Hepatic Tanager
Summer Tanager
Scarlet Tanager
White-winged Tanager
Red-crowned Ant-Tanager
Red-throated Ant-Tanager
Rose-breasted Grosbeak
Blue Bunting
Blue Grosbeak
Indigo Bunting
Painted Bunting
Eastern Meadowlark
Black-cowled Oriole
Orchard Oriole
Yellow-backed Oriole
Yellow-tailed Oriole
Baltimore Oriole
Yellow-billed Cacique
Chestnut-headed Oropendola
Montezuma Oropendola
Yellow-throated Euphonia
Elegant Euphonia
Olive-backed Euphonia
Blue-crowned Chlorophonia

Yellow-winged Tanager

Lake Apanas
(*Lago de Apanás*)

Site Description:

Lake Apanas, Nicaragua's largest artificial lake, was created by damming the water of the Tuma River in the Apanas Valley. This reservoir was developed to provide electric power to much of the country.

The lake is only ten minutes from Jinotega off of the main highway and a dirt road goes around the entire reservoir. The lake provides habitat for a wide range of water-dependant birds and is located near El Jaguar Reserve and Cerro Datanli, which contain many forest specialists.

Directions:

The south shore of the reservoir is located off of the main highway heading northwest out of Jinotega. At the turn off for El Jaguar Reserve (see information for previous site), a dirt road parallels the north shore of the lake. The turn off towards Cerro Datanli follows the south shore of the lake (see site information for directions).

Access/Accommodations:

Arrangements for boat rental can be made with local fishermen or through El Jaguar Reserve. They will make arrangements for a tour with a local fisherman and provide a guide to bird the shallow waters and surrounding wetlands.

Contact Information:

The following contact information is for El Jaguar Reserve that works with a local fisherman to provide tours of Lake Apanas.

Phone: 2279-9219 505 279 9219 • 88 61 016
Email: georges.duriaux@gmail.com
Website: www.jaguarreserve.org (for directions and information)

Description of Birding Sites:

Lake Apanas is an interesting birding site in that birds normally found along the large inland lakes are attracted to this site in the Northern Highlands.

Birding of the shoreline can be done from the highway and area roads where they follow close to the lakeshore. The best birding is done by boat, taking a half-day tour of the open water and surrounding wetland areas.

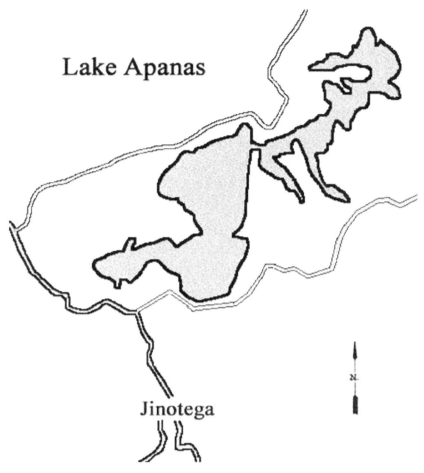

Lake Apanas

Jinotega

Birds of Lake Apanas:

Fulvous Whistling-Duck
Blue-winged Teal
Ring-necked Duck
Neotropic Cormorant
Great Egret
Great Blue Heron
Tricolored Heron
Little Blue Heron
Green Heron
Osprey
White-tailed Kite

Red-tailed Hawk
Common Moorhen
American Coot
Northern Jacana
Spotted Sandpiper
Laughing Gull
Caspian Tern
Ringed Kingfisher
Mangrove Swallow
Northern Rough-winged Swallow
Barn Swallow

180

San Rafael Oak/Pine Forest
Volcan Yali Reserve

Site Description:

Just outside of the town of San Rafael del Norte and within Cerro Yali Reserve lies some of Nicaragua's most accessible montane oak-pine forest. This unusual forest community is found along the drier mid-elevation slopes of Central America and reaches its southern limit in the mountains of northern Nicaragua.

This site is located about 30 minutes north of Jinotega, just off of a dirt road that passes through grazeland with forested slopes. This unusual forest harbors several familiar species of birds, such as resident populations of Red-tailed Hawk, American Kestrel, Northern Flicker, and Eastern Bluebird. It also provides winter habitat for several rare warblers, such as Golden-cheeked and Townsend's.

Directions:

From Jinotega, take the highway north to the town of San Rafael del Norte. Follow the road through the village to the far end where it becomes a dirt road leading toward Yali. From here, the road climbs up into the highlands where forest remnants remain.

Follow this road for 5 km going past the town dump and the canopy tours. On the right side of the road you will see a gate closing off a two-wheel dirt road leading across a field and uphill. Park along the side of the road and walk the dirt road beyond the gate.

This road serves several of the farms beyond, and therefore is available to public access. Be sure to close the gate behind you. Follow this road to the fork, about 150 meters in and then continue to the left. Hike the next 2 to 3 km uphill through open oak and pine forest.

Access/Accommodations:

Stay in Jinotega or undertake this as a day trip from El Jaguar or other nearby reserves where food and lodging are offered.

Contact Information:

Contact information is for El Jaguar Reserve, which can provide a guided tour of the area.a Nebliselva El Jaguar

Phone: 2279-9219 505 279 9219 • 88 61 016
Email: georges.duriaux@gmail.com
Website: www.jaguarreserve.org (for more information)

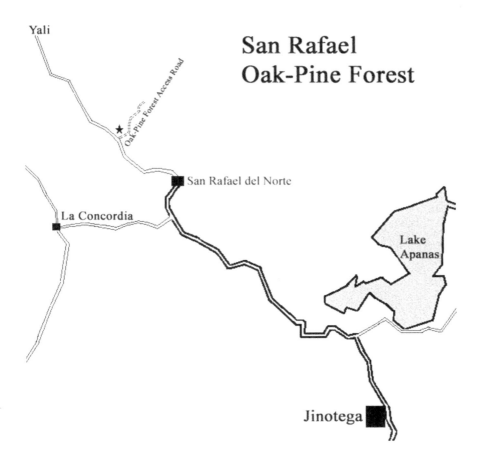

Description of Birding Sites:

The best access to the oak-pine forest is along a dirt road that ascends the hills, located 5 km from San Rafael. Much of the surrounding farmland is private property, however there is a public dirt road that winds up into the surrounding hills and eventually reaches a stand of cloud forest. This road is not hard to find, but is not readily distinguished from other private roads. The staff at El Jaguar provides guided hikes to this area and can also provide information for hiking this road on your own.

Birds of the area:

The resident white-breasted form of the Sharp-shinned Hawk and the "Red-throated" Parakeet (a possible split from Green Parakeet) can be found here. This unique forest community contains a number of species not commonly found in other parts of the country.

Birds of the Oak-Pine Forest:

Cooper's Hawk
Red-tailed Hawk
American Kestrel
Acorn Woodpecker
Hairy Woodpecker
Northern Flicker
White-throated Flycatcher
Olive-sided Flycatcher
Least Flycatcher

Philadelphia Vireo
Blue-headed Vireo
Eastern Bluebird
Black-and-white Warbler
Magnolia Warbler
Black-throated Green Warbler
Blue-black Grassquit
White-collared Seedeater
Lesser Goldfinch

Specialty birds:

Sharp-shinned Hawk (white-breasted race)
Green Parakeet (red-throated race)
Great Swallow-tailed Swift
Azure-crowned Hummingbird
White-eared Hummingbird
Acorn Woodpecker
Greater Pewee
Hermit Warbler
Townsend's Warbler

Golden-cheeked Warbler
Yellow-throated Warbler
Palm Warbler
Painted Redstart
Cinnamon-bellied Flowerpiercer
Hepatic Tanager
Red Crossbill
Black-headed Siskin

Miraflor Natural Reserve
(*Reserva Natural Miraflor*)

Site Description:

Miraflor Reserve measures 25,400 hectares (62,750 acres) and covers three different major habitats; dry forest, semi-decidious forest, and cloud forest. The area ranges in altitude from 800 to 1,484 meters (2,625 to 4,865 feet). The highest point is at Bosque Los Volcancitos.

Miraflor covers a large area, but the forest is somewhat fragmented. As a result, forest interior bird species of the Northern Highlands can be difficult to find, but there is a wide range of birds inhabiting the area with 305 recorded species. This is also one of the richest places in the world for orchids with 200 recorded species.

Miraflor was designated as a reserve in 1990. Similar to several other large reserves in Nicaragua, the land is privately owned and cooperatively managed. This reserve contains nine communities and about 7,000 people live in the reserve making a living from farming.

The reserve is almost entirely self-funded by associations of small scale producers. A local foundation works with area farmers on improving farming techniques to be more sustainable. Among the various crops grown here, coffee is the most important.

Because of the relatively high elevation, the climate is rather mild with cool nights and even cold temperatures at high elevations. The reserve is comprised of a mix of woodlands and open fields and provides good opportunities for hiking and birding.

Directions/Access:

Miraflor is located 32 km from Esteli along a gravel road. It will take around 45 mintues to reach the area by car. The road to Miraflor is bumpy and gets dusty during the dry season. A high clearance car is recommended.

Coming from Jinotega, drive towards San Rafael and turn to La Concordia. From La Concordia, turn right to take the road north to Miraflor (the road to the south goes to Esteli. You will enter the reserve just north of the village. Going straight from La Concordia will lead you down a very poor dirt road with sparse habitat and limited birding.

Public Transportation: Buses to Miraflor leave from Managua and Esteli. From Managua it will take two to three hours to reach the reserve. Additional information about local transporation is available at the UCA Miraflor office (Union of Cooperative Agriculture) in Estelí.

There are four buses per day departing Esteli. Two buses leave for La Pita, at 6 a.m. and 1 p.m, from the Pulpería Miraflor located by the Texaco Starmart at the north end of town. The buses to Sontule and La Perla leave from COTRAN Norte at 2 p.m. and 3:40 p.m.

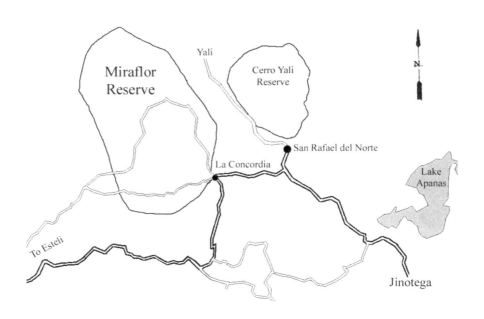

Access/Accommodations:

Accommodations for visitors are available at many of the area farms. The housing offered is very simple and back-to-basic, with no electricity in your room or running water. Another option is to stay at Finca Neblina del Bosque Lodge (see below).

Hours of operation:

When visiting Miraflor Reserve be sure to make a reservation through the office in Estelí before you head off to Miraflor. Here you can arrange for rooms, guides and other services.

Contact Information:

Phone: 2713-2971 (Miraflor office in Esteli)
Email: miraflor@ibw.com.ni or miraflor@cablenet.com.ni
Website: www.miraflor.org

Rufous-tailed Hummingbird

Finca Neblina del Bosque Ecolodge

Site Description: Finca Neblina del Bosque is both a working farm and ecolodge that has been developed within Miraflor Reserve. The farm is run by a Nicaraguan/German couple, Eduardo and Isabel. They provide bamboo cabins with panoramic views and solar powered lighting.

Directions:

In Esteli, drive to the Uno gas station (#2 on the north end of the city). Turn right onto a gravel road and follow this for 32 km to reach the lodge. It will take about 45 to 60 minutes to get there. A four-wheel drive vehicle is required to reach the ecolodge.

Public Transportation: Buses leave from the Cotran Norte Bus terminal in Esteli at 6:00 am, noon and 3:40 pm to Miraflor. Buses will arrive at the La Rampa bus stop. From here it is a 300 meter walk to the lodge. Finca Neblina del Bosque is at the top of the hill on the right.

Access/Accommodations:

Several rooms are available at the lodge and range from $25 per person with up to four to a cabin. The price includes three meals.

A variety of tours are available, ranging from two to eight hours and focus on the birds, orchids and other aspects of the area. The cost for a bilingual guide is $15 to $25 per day, depending on the duration. A guide may also accompany visitors from Esteli upon reservation.

Contact: www.naturereservemiraflor.com

Description of Birding Sites:

Birding can be done along any of the dirt roads that connect the local farms and several hiking trails have been developed, particularly at Neblina del Bosque Lodge.

Birds of Miraflor Reserve

Great Tinamou
Little Tinamou
Black-bellied Whistling-Duck
American Wigeon
Mallard
Plain Chachalaca
Crested Bobwhite
Least Grebe
Pied-billed Grebe
Wood Stork
Great Blue Heron
Great Egret
Snowy Egret
Little Blue Heron
Tricolored Heron
Cattle Egret
Green Heron
Osprey
White-tailed Kite
Hook-billed Kite
Swallow-tailed Kite
Snail Kite
Mississippi Kite
Northern Harrier
Tiny Hawk
Bicolored Hawk
Crane Hawk
Great Black-Hawk
Roadside Hawk
Broad-winged Hawk
Gray Hawk
Short-tailed Hawk
Zone-tailed Hawk
Red-tailed Hawk
Gray-necked Wood-Rail
Common Moorhen
Killdeer
Northern Jacana
Spotted Sandpiper
Solitary Sandpiper

Least Sandpiper
Red-billed Pigeon
Band-tailed Pigeon
White-winged Dove
Mourning Dove
Inca Dove
Common Ground-Dove
Ruddy Ground-Dove
Blue Ground-Dove
White-tipped Dove
Gray-fronted Dove
White-faced Quail-Dove
Squirrel Cuckoo
Yellow-billed Cuckoo
Mangrove Cuckoo
Black-billed Cuckoo
Striped Cuckoo
Groove-billed Ani
Barn Owl
Vermiculated Screech-Owl
Ferruginous Pygmy-Owl
Stygian Owl
Lesser Nighthawk
Common Pauraque
Whip-poor-will
White-collared Swift
Vaux's Swift
Lesser Swallow-tailed Swift
Great Swallow-tailed Swift
Bronzy Hermit
Long-billed Hermit
Little Hermit
Brown Violetear
Green Violetear
Green-breasted Mango
Long-billed Starthroat
Plain-capped Starthroat
Green-breasted Mountain-gem
Ruby-throated Hummingbird
Canivet's Emerald

Violet Sabrewing
Stripe-tailed Hummingbird
Blue-chested Hummingbird
Blue-tailed Hummingbird
Rufous-tailed Hummingbird
Cinnamon Hummingbird
Gartered Trogon
Elegant Trogon
Collared Trogon
Blue-crowned Motmot
Turquoise-browed Motmot
Belted Kingfisher
Amazon Kingfisher
Green Kingfisher
Rufous-tailed Jacamar
Emerald Toucanet
Collared Aracari
Acorn Woodpecker
Hoffmann's Woodpecker
Smoky-brown Woodpecker
Hairy Woodpecker
Golden-olive Woodpecker
Northern Flicker
Lineated Woodpecker
Pale-billed Woodpecker
Barred Forest-Falcon
Collared Forest-Falcon
Crested Caracara
Laughing Falcon
American Kestrel
Bat Falcon
Orange-fronted Parakeet
Orange-chinned Parakeet
White-crowned Parrot
White-fronted Parrot
Barred Antshrike
Slaty Antwren
Dot-winged Antwren
Dusky Antwren
Black-faced Antthrush
Olivaceous Woodcreeper
Ruddy Woodcreeper

No. Barred Woodcreeper
Strong-billed Woodcreeper
Spotted Woodcreeper
Plain Xenops
Yellow-bellied Elaenia
Ochre-bellied Flycatcher
Sepia-capped Flycatcher
Slate-headed Tody-Flycatcher
Common Tody-Flycatcher
Eye-ringed Flatbill
Yellow-olive Flycatcher
Stub-tailed Spadebill
Tufted Flycatcher
Greater Pewee
Tropical Pewee
White-throated Flycatcher
Yellowish Flycatcher
Black Phoebe
Bright-rumped Attila
Dusky-capped Flycatcher
Great Crested Flycatcher
Brown-crested Flycatcher
Boat-billed Flycatcher
Gray-capped Flycatcher
Sulphur-bellied Flycatcher
Piratic Flycatcher
Western Kingbird
Scissor-tailed Flycatcher
Fork-tailed Flycatcher
Long-tailed Manakin
Black-crowned Tityra
Masked Tityra
Gray-collared Becard
Yellow-throated Vireo
Blue-headed Vireo
Yellow-green Vireo
Lesser Greenlet
Rufous-browed Peppershrike
White-throated Magpie-Jay
Brown Jay
No. Rough-winged Swallow
So. Rough-winged Swallow

Purple Martin
Mangrove Swallow
Barn Swallow
Cliff Swallow
Rock Wren
House Wren
Band-backed Wren
Rufous-naped Wren
Spot-breasted Wren
Banded Wren
Rufous-and-white Wren
Plain Wren
Long-billed Gnatwren
Tropical Gnatcatcher
Eastern Bluebird
Orange-billed Nightingale-Thrush
Swainson's Thrush
Wood Thrush
Clay-colored Thrush
Gray Catbird
Tropical Mockingbird
Cedar Waxwing
Ovenbird
Worm-eating Warbler
Louisiana Waterthrush
Northern Waterthrush
Blue-winged Warbler
Golden-winged Warbler
Black-and-white Warbler
Crescent-chested Warbler
Tennessee Warbler
Gray-crowned Yellowthroat
MacGillivray's Warbler
Kentucky Warbler
Common Yellowthroat
American Redstart
Cerulean Warbler
Tropical Parula
Magnolia Warbler
Yellow Warbler
Bay-breasted Warbler
Chestnut-sided Warbler

Yellow-rumped Warbler
Townsend's Warbler
Black-throated Green Warbler
Fan-tailed Warbler
Rufous-capped Warbler
Golden-crowned Warbler
Canada Warbler
Wilson's Warbler
Painted Redstart
Crimson-collared Tanager
Passerini's Tanager
Golden-hooded Tanager
Rufous-winged Tanager
Cinnamon-bellied Flowerpiercer
Blue-black Grassquit
Variable Seedeater
White-collared Seedeater
Yellow-faced Grassquit
Grayish Saltator
Buff-throated Saltator
Black-headed Saltator
Chestnut-capped Brush-Finch
Black-striped Sparrow
White-naped Brush-Finch
Rusty Sparrow
White-eared Ground-Sparrow
Stripe-headed Sparrow
Common Bush-Tanager
Hepatic Tanager
Summer Tanager
Scarlet Tanager
Western Tanager
Flame-colored Tanager
White-winged Tanager
Red-crowned Ant-Tanager
Rose-breasted Grosbeak
Blue Seedeater
Blue-black Grosbeak
Blue Bunting
Blue Grosbeak
Indigo Bunting
Painted Bunting

191

Eastern Meadowlark
Melodious Blackbird
Bronzed Cowbird
Giant Cowbird
Black-vented Oriole
Orchard Oriole
Yellow-backed Oriole
Streak-backed Oriole
Spot-breasted Oriole
Altamira Oriole

Baltimore Oriole
Yellow-billed Cacique
Chestnut-headed Oropendola
Montezuma Oropendola
Yellow-crowned Euphonia
Yellow-throated Euphonia
Elegant Euphonia
Blue-crowned Chlorophonia
Black-headed Siskin
Lesser Goldfinch

Specialty Birds:

Thicket Tinamou
Slaty-breasted Tinamou
Highland Guan
Great Curassow
Buffy-crowned Wood-Quail
Gray-headed Kite
Ornate Hawk-Eagle
Ruddy Crake
Ruddy Quail-Dove
Pheasant Cuckoo
Lesser Ground-Cuckoo
Lesser Roadrunner
Azure-crowned Hummingbird

White-eared Hummingbird
Resplendent Quetzal
Scaled Antpitta
Slaty Spinetail
Three-wattled Bellbird
Bushy-crested Jay
White-breasted Wood-Wren
Slate-colored Solitaire
Black-headed Nightingale-Thrush
Mountain Thrush
White-throated Thrush
Blue-and-white Mockingbird
Yellow-winged Tanager

Wood Thrush

Additional Sites

Esperanza Verde Reserve
(*Reserva Silvestre Privada Esperanza Verde*)

Site Description:

This reserve recently changed hands, and its current status is uncertain. Please check for updated information before making plans to visit. The following information was current in 2011.

Finca Esperanza Verde is an eco-lodge, coffee farm, and private reserve 3 hours from Managua located on 23 hectares (56 acres) of land. Finca Esperanza Verde was founded in 1998 by Durham-San Ramon Sister Communities and is a community-based project run by volunteers from North Carolina with an all-Nicaraguan staff. The organization's aim is to have a sustainable and environmentally-friendly farm and reserve. The results can be seen in the solar-powering of the farm, the spring-fed water supply and the organic shade-grown coffee production. In 2004 it received a Sustainable Tourism Award from the Smithsonian Magazine.

Visitors can hike the forests surrounding the farm in search of the more than 150 species of birds that have been recorded here. A bird feeding station has also been established at the reserve. There are hiking trails leading to local waterfalls and a picnic site. Rental of a truck and driver is also possible and there is a butterfly farm you can visit as well.

Lodging at Finca Esperanze Verde is a rural experience on the edge of forests and coffee plantations, and accommodations are rustic. Both the farm and lodge have been developed to be as eco-friendly as possible with minimal impact to the land.

Directions:

Finca Esperanza Verde is located 30 km from Matagalpa, at an elevation of 1,200 meters in the mountainous and forested region in the northern part of Nicaragua. By car, take the road from Matagalpa to La Dalia. After about 25 minutes from Matagalpa you will see signs to San Ramon. Finca Esperanza Verde is 50 minutes over gravel roads from San Ramon and can be done with a two-wheel drive. In Yucul, turn left off of the main road and follow the signs toward Finca Esperanza Verde.

Public Transportation: There is a bus from Matagalpa that passes through San Ramon and towards Pancasan and to El Jobo. Get off at Yucul, located about 40 minutes from Matagalpa. You will need to hike uphill about one hour from Yucul to Finca Esperanza Verde. Follow the signs along the road.

Access/Accommodations:

The eco-lodge has 5 cabins with space for 22 people. Camping is allowed for $6 per night and cabins range from $10 to $45 per night. Prices may vary depending on the season. The lodge also serves meals, made on the site using locally grown products. The entrance fee for day visitors is $3.

Contact Information:

Phone: 2772-5003 or try 2583-0127 (Mabel Martínez)
or 2850-9388 (Mario Obando)
Email: herma@ibw.com.ni
Website: www.fincaesperanzaverde.org or
www.avesnicaragua.org/EsperanzaVerde.htm

Trails:

The reserve contains 3 trails and 5 km total trail length. The trails are of moderate difficulty and generally easy walking.

Peñas Blancas Natural Reserve
(*Reserva Natural Peñas Blancas*)

Peñas Blancas is part of the Bosawás Biosphere Reserve, lying on its western edge on the border between the provinces of Jinotega and Matagalpa. Due to its location in the Northern Highlands, it has been included in this section of the book. This reserve was established in 1999 for the purpose of watershed protection and to protect the primary forest. This reserve lies at the headwaters of several of Nicaragua's major rivers.

The Peñas Blancas Massif is named for the white cliff-like walls of rock that rise from the earth. This area is noted for its tall mountains, including one of the country's highest at 1,745 meters (5,725 feet) above sea level, plus numerous waterfalls, cloud forest, and rainforest.

The area is inhabited by rural, small-scale farmers with small settlements scattered throughout the region. Lodging is available in some of the area communities. Currently, there is one eco-lodge in the village of Peñas Blancas, or it is possible to stay at the homes of farmers here and in Valle de los Lyra. It is also possible to camp in the reserve.

This is a very remote site with few developments. However, there are several trails through the forest. All hikes should be undertaken with a local guide, which runs around $5 per person.

Peñas Blancas is located about 60 km from Matagalpa (around 200 km from Managua). The reserve can be reached from Matagalpa in about 2 hours. From Matagalpa, take the road to El Tuma and La Dalia. At La Dalia, head towards El Cuá to reach the village of Peñas Blancas. For information, stop at Km 195 on the road to El Cuá to reach "Centro del Entrendimiento de la Naturaleza". A four-wheel drive is necessary to travel here.

For more information:
Website www.vianica.com

Conservation

Similar to every other country, Nicaragua has its environmental problems and endangered species. The ultimate source for wildlife problems is human activities—habitat destruction, pollution, invasive species, etc. While habitat destruction is among the greatest concerns, it is also the scale and pace at which this is proceeding as compared to conservation efforts to protect and manage wildlife habitat. In Nicaragua it is still relatively low compared to other countries, but certainly a concern. Among the greatest impact comes from deforestation and poor agricultural practices. The degree of impact that pesticides are having on these lands and waterways is still largely unknown for this region.

Nicaragua has a number of challenges to conservation, but is making an effort to protect a number of important habitat areas. Perhaps due to the poor ecomony, there has been a lack of development. Also due to the inhospital nature of the Atlantic Lowlands, much of this area remains as a relatively large, intact tropical forest ecosystem at this time.

Among the most threatened habitats are the dry tropical forests, oak-pine forests, cloud forest, and mangroves. The primary cause for land conversion in these ecosystems is agriculture. In the dry tropical forests and oak-pine forests changes are coming from fruit and vegetable production as well as from cattle and other grazing animals. In the cloud forest, the important economic products of coffee and cattle are resulting in the loss of habitat. Mangrove forests are being lost as in other coastal areas worldwide due to development.

Of the more than 700 bird species known to Nicaragua, several of them are identified as threatened or endangered. Nicaragua has signed the CITES Treaty (Convention on International Trade of Endangered Species) and recognizes a number of listed species.

CITES I Status:	8 species
CITES II Status:	97 species
CITES III	7 species

In another analysis of the status of birds in Nicaragua, the International Union for the Conservation of Nature (IUCN – Birdlife International) has listed the following:

Critically Endangered	1 species
Endangered	2 species
Vulnerable	11 species
Near Threatened	20 species
Species of Least Concern	641 species

The Galapagos Petrel (Shearwater) is listed as critically endangered, but is only a vagrant in the waters off of Nicaragua.

Endangered birds:

Great Green Macaw
Golden-cheeked Warbler

Great Green Macaw occurs from Honduras to northwest Colombia, with a separate subspecies in Ecuador. Currently, the largest remaining population occurs in southern Nicaragua. This is a bird of the lowland tropical forest that has been severely impacted by habitat destruction throughout much of its range. The main causes are from banana and pineapple agriculture and cattle ranching, but also include the illegal pet trade and illegal harvesting of high-value almendro trees.

The Golden-cheeked Warbler consists of a small breeding population found in central Texas. It was only recently rediscovered wintering in the highlands of Nicaragua, and studies are underway to determine the extent of the population and critical habitat areas.

Vulnerable birds:

Great Curassow	Yellow-naped Amazon (Parrot)
Highland Guan	Tawny-chested Flycatcher
Ocellated Quail	Keel-billed Motmot
Agami Heron	Three-wattled Bellbird
	Cerulean Warbler

This list also includes Pink-footed Shearwater, which is not currently listed for Nicaragua, but is likely to occur in off-shore waters. Also included is Parkinson's Petrel, or Black Petrel, which is not known for Nicaragua. The Great Currassow and Highland Guan are sought after for food through illegal hunting, and habitat loss are the greatest threats. The Yellow-naped Amazon (Yellow-naped Parrot) is largely threatened by the pet trade, both locally and internationally.

Near Threatened:

Great Tinamou	Elegant Tern
Reddish Egret	White-crowned Pigeon
Harpy Eagle	Chimney Swift
Solitary Eagle	Long-tailed Woodcreeper
Crested Eagle	Resplendent Quetzal
Ornate Hawk-eagle	Olive-sided Flycatcher
Orange-breasted Falcon	Wing-banded Antbird
Piping Plover	Bell's Vireo
Semipalmated Sandpiper	Golden-winged Warbler
Buff-breasted Sandpiper	Painted Bunting

In summary, while IUCN has developed a comprehensive list of threatened and endangered species for Nicaragua, they only identify 675 species for the country. Among those listed are Galapagos Petrel (Shearwater), which is of very rare occurrence, and Parkinson's Petrel (Black Petrel), which has not been recorded in Nicaragua.

And while the Galapagos Shearwater has been recorded in the coastal and nearby open waters, Nicaragua does not provide critical habitat for this species. Among others included on the list of threatened species, some are possibly being impacted by environmental factors outside of Nicaragua that affect their breeding grounds, such as Chimney Swift, Cerulean Warbler, Olive-sided Flycatcher and Bell's Vireo, although the true causes for their decline is yet to be determined. Also, Reddish Egret is the least common of the egret species known to Nicaragua, so while it is a vulnerable species, the problems tend to arise more from the core of its range.

On the other hand, Nicaragua's Northern Highlands provide important over-wintering habitat for the Golden-winged Warbler, and better land management practices may be essential to its recovery. And while Nicargua does list several species of birds as game species, enforcement of regulations is minimal, similar to the lack of controls on taking birds from the wild for the pet trade

Of particular concern is the status of the Yellow-naped Parrot. It is threatened by habitat loss and illegal trade in the pet industry. Taking birds from the wild as pets is illegal under Nicaragua's laws, but there is no enforcement and keeping parakeets, parrots and macaws as pets is widespread and a strong cultural tradition. Additionally, several species of orioles and tanagers are occasionally solicited for sale, and even species such as oropendulas are vulnerable.

As a result, a number of species are being captured from the wild, at varying degrees of intensity, for profit through sales to both residents and foreigners. Although none of this has been quantified in any way, the pervasiveness of capturing wild birds is currently a significant threat to several species.

Finally, while Nicaragua has designated a wide range of nature reserves, including such vast areas as the Bosawas Reserve, which encompasses 15% of the land area of the country, these lands are not publically owned. Instead they rely on cooperative management with landowners and farmers in the area and as a result economic pressures are often in conflict with management needs.

However, there is an increasing number of formally protected areas in Nicaragua that encompass a wide range of landscapes and important habitats. They also total an impressive number of acres. In order to be functional as protected areas, they will require governmental support and adequate funding and staffing, along with effective enforcement of regulations that are meant to provide the intended protection for Nicaragua's wildlife and their habitats

Captive Orange-fronted Parakeet
(Note the trimmed flight feathers)

Overall, habitat loss and land conversion is the greatest threat to wildlife in Nicaragua as elsewhere. The loss of important habitat areas or degradation of these lands, which limit opportunities for many species, affects not only the resident birds in Nicaragua, but also impacts the over-wintering sites for North America breeding species. It is for this reason that numerous conservation efforts throughout Central America, the Caribbean Islands and northern South America are being coordinated and funded by organizations and agencies in the United States and Canada.

Hopefully, these combined efforts along with a greater awareness of the ecological and economic importance of wildlife to Nicaraguans will be sufficient to keep pace with the rate of change to the land and consequently wildlife populations. It is my personal hope that con-servation efforts will result in there always being places in Nicaragua and other countries where birders can go to watch and enjoy birds.

National Parks and Protected Areas

Nicaragua possesses a system of Protected Areas that shelters a wide range of ecosystems that includes thousands of species of flora and fauna. To date, there are about 12,000 species of plants known to the country and more than 1, 400 species of animals.

Most Important Protected Areas:

Bosawas Biosphere Reserve—the biggest Central American rainforest.
Indio-Maiz Biological Reserve
Juan Venado Island Natural Reserve
Los Gatuzos Wildlife Refuge
Maderas Volcano
Masaya Volcano National Park
Miraflor Natural Reserve
Miskitos Cays Biological Reserve
Mombacho Volcano Reserve
Rio Escalante Chacocente Wildlife
Zapatera Archipelago National Park—archeological site.

For more information see:

http://www.centralamerica.com/nigaragua/parks/nationalpark.htm

Natural Reserves in Nicaragua

Chocoyero – El Brujo Natural Reserve	Chocoyero
Montibelli Private Nature Reserve	Ticuantepe
Selva Negra Private Nature Reserve	Matagalpa
Charco Verde	Ometepe Island
La Flor Sea Turtle Reserve	San Juan del Sur
La Primavera Private Wildlife Reserve	San Juan del Sur
El Jaguar Nature Reserve	Jinotega
Esperanza Verde Nature Reserve	San Carlos
Los Guatuzos Wildlife Refuge	San Carlos
Somoto Canyon	Somoto
Miraflor Natural Reserve	Miraflor
Cantagallo Ecological Park	Condega
La Pataste Natural Reserve	Pueblo Nuevo
Islotes de Cosigüina	Golfo Fonseca
Kilambé Massif Natural Reserve	Wiwilí
Cerro Arenal Natural Reserve	Arenal
Indio Maíz Biological Reserve	Indio Maíz
Wawashang Natural Reserve	Laguna de Perlas
Peñas Blancas Massif	Peñas Blancas
Apante Hill	Matagalpa

Volcanoes

Cosigüina Volcano	Chinangeda
El Chonco	Chinandega
San Cristobal	Chinandega
Casita	Chinandega
Telíca Volcano	Leon
Rota	Leon
Cerro Negro Volcano	Leon
Momotombo Volcano	Managua
Volcán Masaya Volcano National Park	Nindirí
Mombacho Volcano	Granada
Maderas Volcano	Isla de Ometepe
Concepción Volcano	Isla de Ometepe

Important Bird Areas
(IBA's) in Nicaragua

N 1001	Farallones de Cosisguina
N1002	Volcan Cosiguina
N1003	Delta del Estero Real y Llanos de Apacunca
N1004	Complejo Volcanico San Critobal-Casita
N1005	Complejo Volcanico Momotombo
N1006	Humedales de Norte del Lago de Managua
N1007	Chocoyero-El Bruo y paisaje aledano
N1008	Rio Escaalante-Cecocente-Tecomapa
N1009	Laguna de Tisma
N1010	Volcan Mombacho
N1011	Domitila
N1012	Volcan Maderas
N1013	Cordellera Dipilito-Jalapa
N1014	Miraflor
N1015	El Jaguar
N1016	Cerro Datanli-El Diablo
N1017	Cerro Arenal
N1018	Cerro Kilambe
N1019	Macizo Penas Blancas
N1020	Serrania de Quirragua y paisaje aledano
N1021	Cerro Musun
N1022	Archipelago Solentiname
N1023	Los Guatuzos
N1024	Bosawas
N1025	Cayos Miskitos y paisaje terrestre
N1026	Rios Prinzapolka/Alamikamba
N1027	Wawashan
N1028	Bahia de Bluefields y paisaje alendano
N1029	Cerro Silva
N1030	Punta Gorda
N1031	Isla Booby Cay
N1032	Indio Maiz
N1033	Rio San Juan- La Inmaculada Concepcion de Maria

Nicaragua's Important Bird Areas

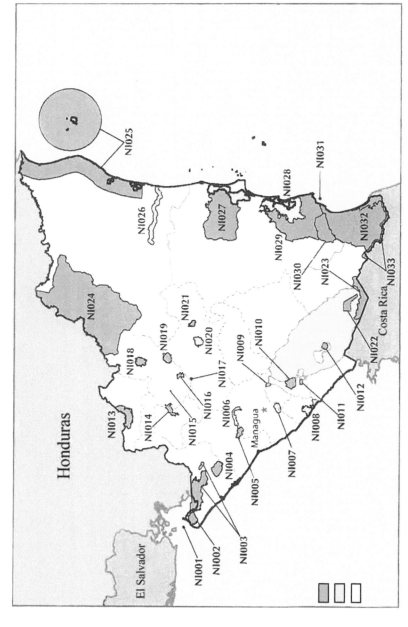

Ramsar Sites
Wetlands of International Importance:

Nicaraguais is a signatory of the Ramsar Convention. The Convention on Wetlands (Ramsar, Iran, 1971)—called the "Ramsar Convention"—is an intergovernmental treaty that embodies the commitments of its member countries to maintain the ecological character of their Wetlands of International Importance and to plan for the "wise use", or sustainable use, of all of the wetlands in their territories.

As of 2013, Nicaragua has nine designated Ramsar Sites, or Wetlands of International Importance.

1. Cayos Miskitos y Franja Costera Immediata
2. Deltas del Estero Real y Llanos de Apacunca
3. Lago de Apanás-Asturias
4. Los Guatuzos
5. Refugio de Vida Silvestre Río San Juan
6. Sistema de Humedales de la Bahía de Bluefields
7. Sistema de Humedales de San Miguelito
8. Sistema Lagunar de Tisma
9. Sistema Lacustre Playitas, Moyúa-Tecomapa

Checklist of the
Birds of Nicaragua

This checklist follows the 6th edition of Clement's Checklist of the Birds of the World, 2011. The information was largely taken from the most recent comprehensive checklist of the birds of Nicaragua by Juan Carlos Martinez Sanchez, et. al., 2007 in which 708 known species are listed. Since then, another 41 confirmed species have been added, bringing the total checklist to 749 species of birds in 74 families known to Nicaragua as of 2013.

In recent years the taxonomy of the birds of this region, as well as throughout much of the world, has undergone a dramatic revision. Many species have been re-classified and renamed. I have tried to include all of these recent changes in both common and scientific names and list the birds in the most recent family and species order. I checked the classification and names of the species against several references and reviewed this checklist as thoroughly as I can. While others have reviewed this list for its accuracy and completeness, any errors are entirely my own. Any corrections, changes, or suggestions are willingly accepted in order to maintain its usefulness and keep it current.

Vagrant or accidental species are indicated with an asterisk.

I also have developed a daily checklist of the birds of Nicaragua, which is available wherever this book is sold. This is an initial effort to develop a comprehensive bird checklist for Nicaragua designed for birders from the U.S. and for other English-speaking birders and field ornithologists. This checklist has been developed with spaces to record ten days of daily sightings.

Acknowledgments: I extend my appreciation to the following for their input and review: Juan Carlos Martinez-Sanchez, Jose Manuel Zolotoff-Pallais, Salvadora Morales, Lilliana Chavarria, and Manfred Bienert. Also, thanks to Noel Cutright and Sumner Matteson for reviewing the final draft.

Tinamous: (4 species)
___ Great Tinamou .... *Tinamus major*
___ Little Tinamou .... *Crypturellus soui*
___ Slaty-breasted Tinamou .... *Crypturellus boucardi*
___ Thicket Tinamou .... *Crypturellus cinnamomeus*

Ducks, Geese and Swans: (17 species)
___ Black-bellied Whistling-Duck .... *Dendrocygna autumnalis*
___ Fulvous Whistling-Duck .... *Dendrocygna bicolor*
___ Muscovy Duck .... *Cairina moschata*
___ American Wigeon .... *Anas americana*
___ Mallard .... *Anas platyrhynchos*
___ Blue-winged Teal .... *Anas discors*
___ Cinnamon Teal .... *Anas cyanoptera*
___ Northern Shoveler .... *Anas clypeata*
___ Northern Pintail .... *Anas acuta*
___ Green-winged Teal .... *Anas crecca*
___ Canvasback .... *Aythya valisineria*
___ Redhead .... *Aythya americana*
___ Ring-necked Duck .... *Aythya collaris*
___ Greater Scaup .... *Aythya marila*
___ Lesser Scaup .... *Aythya affinis*
___ Masked Duck .... *Nomonyx dominicus*
___ Ruddy Duck .... *Oxyura jamaicensis*

Guans, Curassows & Chachalacas: (6 species)
___ Plain Chachalaca .... *Ortalis vetula*
___ Gray-headed Chachalaca .... *Ortalis cinereiceps*
___ White-bellied Chachalaca .... *Ortalis leucogastra*
___ Crested Guan .... *Penelope purpurascens*
___ Highland Guan .... *Penelopina nigra*
___ Great Curassow .... *Crax rubra*

Partridge & Quails: (8 species)
___ Buffy-crowned Wood-Partridge .... *Dendrortyx leucophrys*
___ Black-throated Bobwhite .... *Colinus nigrogularis*
___ Crested Bobwhite .... *Colinus cristatus*
___ Spot-bellied Bobwhite .... *Colinus leucopogon*
___ Black-eared Wood-Quail .... *Odontophorus melanotis*
___ Spotted Wood-Quail .... *Odontophorus guttatus*
___ Ocellated Quail .... *Cyrtonyx ocellatus*

__ Tawny-faced Quail   *Rhynchortyx cinctus*

Grebes: (2 species)
__ Least Grebe   *Tachybaptus dominicus*
__ Pied-billed Grebe   *Podilymbus podiceps*

Shearwaters and Petrels: (3 species)
__ Black-capped Petrel   *Pterodroma hasiata*
__ * Wedge-tailed Shearwater   *Puffinus pacificus*
__ * Galapagos Shearwater   *Puffinus subalaris*

Storm-Petrels: (4 species)
__ Leach's Storm-Petrel   *Oceanodroma leucorhoa*
__ * Wedge-rumped Storm-Petrel   *Oceanodroma tethys*
__ Black Storm-Petrel   *Oceanodroma melania*
__ Least Storm-Petrel   *Oceanodroma microsoma*

Tropicbirds: (1 species)
__ Red-billed Tropicbird   *Phaethon aethereus*

Storks: (2 species)
__ Jabiru   *Jabiru mycteria*
__ Wood Stork   *Mycteria americana*

Frigatebirds: (1 species)
__ Magnificent Frigatebird   *Fregata magnificens*

Boobies & Gannets: (4 species)
__ Nazca Booby   *Sula granti*
__ Blue-footed Booby   *Sula nebouxii*
__ Brown Booby   *Sula leucogaster*
__ Red-footed Booby   *Sula sula*

Cormorants: (1 species)
__ Neotropic Cormorant   *Phalacrocorax brasilianus*

Anhingas: (1 species)
__ Anhinga   *Anhinga anhinga*

Pelicans: (2 species)
__ American White Pelican   *Pelecanus erythrorhynchos*
__ Brown Pelican   *Pelecanus occidentalis*

Herons, Egrets and Bitterns: (19 species)
__ Pinnated Bittern   *Botaurus pinnatus*
__ American Bittern   *Botaurus lentiginosus*
__ Least Bittern   *Ixobrychus exilis*
__ Rufescent Tiger-Heron   *Tigrisoma lineatum*
__ Faciated Tiger-Heron   *Tigrisoma fasciatum*
__ Bare-throated Tiger-Heron   *Tigrisoma mexicanum*
__ Great Blue Heron   *Ardea herodias*
__ Great Egret   *Ardea alba*
__ Snowy Egret   *Egretta thula*
__ Little Blue Heron   *Egretta caerulea*
__ Tricolored Heron   *Egretta tricolor*
__ Reddish Egret   *Egrettea rufescens*
__ Cattle Egret   *Bubulcus ibis*
__ Striated Heron   *Butorides striata*
__ Green Heron   *Butorides virescens*
__ Agami Heron   *Agamia agami*
__ Black-crowned Night-Heron   *Nycticorax nycticorax*
__ Yellow-crowned Night-Heron   *Nyctanassa violacea*
__ Boat-billed Heron   *Cochlearius cochlearius*

Ibises & Spoonbills: (5 species)
__ White Ibis   *Eudocimus albus*
__ Glossy Ibis   *Plegadis falcinellus*
__ White-faced Ibis   *Plegadis chihi*
__ Green Ibis   *Mesembrinibis cayennensis*
__ Roseate Spoonbill   *Platalea ajaja*

New World Vultures: (4 species)
__ Black Vulture   *Coragyps atratus*
__ Turkey Vulture   *Cathartes aura*
__ Lesser Yellow-headed Vulture   *Cathartes burrovianus*
__ King Vulture   *Sarcoramphus papa*

Osprey: (1 species)
__ Osprey   *Pandion haliaetus*

210

Eagles, Hawks & Kites: (37 species)

__ Pearl Kite	*Gampsonyx swainsonii*
__ White-tailed Kite	*Elanus leucurus*
__ Hook-billed Kite	*Chondrohierax uncinatus*
__ Gray-headed Kite	*Leptodon cayanensis*
__ Swallow-tailed Kite	*Elanoides forficatus*
__ Crested Eagle	*Morphnus guianensis*
__ Harpy Eagle	*Harpia harpyja*
__ Black Hawk-Eagle	*Spizaetus tryannus*
__ Ornate Hawk-Eagle	*Spizaetus ornatus*
__ Black-and-white Hawk-Eagle	*Spizaetus melanoleucus*
__ Black-collared Hawk	*Busarellus nigricollis*
__ Snail Kite	*Rostrhamus sociabilis*
__ Double-toothed Kite	*Harpagus bidentatus*
__ Mississippi Kite	*Ictinia mississippiensis*
__ Plumbeous Kite	*Ictinia plumbea*
__ Northern Harrier	*Circus cyaneus*
__ Tiny Hawk	*Accipiter superciliosus*
__ Sharp-shinned Hawk	*Accipiter striatus*
__ Cooper's Hawk	*Accipiter cooperii*
__ Bicolored Hawk	*Accipiter bicolor*
__ Crane Hawk	*Geranospiza caerulescens*
__ Common Black-Hawk	*Buteogallus anthracinus*
__ * Savanna Hawk	*Buteogallus meridionalis*
__ Great Black-Hawk	*Buteogallus urubitinga*
__ Solitary Eagle	*Buteogallus solitarius*
__ Barred Hawk	*Morphnarchus princeps*
__ Roadside Hawk	*Rupornis magnirostris*
__ Harris's Hawk	*Parabuteo unicinctus*
__ White-tailed Hawk	*Geranoaetus albicaudatus*
__ White Hawk	*Pseudastur albicollis*
__ Semiplumbeous Hawk	*Leucopternis semiplumbeus*
__ Broad-winged Hawk	*Buteo platypterus*
__ Gray Hawk	*Buteo plagiatus*
__ Short-tailed Hawk	*Buteo brachyurus*
__ Swainson's Hawk	*Buteo swainsoni*
__ Zone-tailed Hawk	*Buteo albonotatus*
__ Red-tailed Hawk	*Buteo jamaicensis*

Sunbitterns: (1 species)
__ Sunbittern   *Eurypyga helias*

Rails, Gallinules & Coots: (12 species)
__ Ruddy Crake   *Laterallus ruber*
__ White-throated Crake   *Laterallus albigularis*
__ Gray-breasted Crake   *Laterallus exilis*
__ Rufous-necked Wood-Rail   *Aramides axillaris*
__ Gray-necked Wood-Rail   *Aramides cajaneus*
__ Uniform Crake   *Amaurolimnas concolor*
__ Sora   *Porzana carolina*
__ Yellow-breasted Crake   *Poliomnas flaviventer*
__ Spotted Rail   *Pardirallus maculatus*
__ Purple Gallinule   *Porphyrio martinicus*
__ Common Gallinule   *Gallinula galeata*
__ American Coot   *Fulica americana*

Finfoots: (1 species)
__ Sungrebe   *Heliornis fulica*

Limpkin: (1 species)
__ Limpkin   *Aramus guarauna*

Thick-knees: (1 species)
__ Double-striped Thick-Knee   *Burhinus bistriatus*

Plovers & Lapwings: (10 species)
__ * Southern Lapwing   *Vanellus chilensis*
__ Black-bellied Plover   *Pluvialis squatarola*
__ American Golden Plover   *Pluvialis dominica*
__ * Pacific Golden Plover   *Pluvialis fulva*
__ Collared Plover   *Charadrius collaris*
__ Snowy Plover   *Charadrius nivosus*
__ Wilson's Plover   *Charadrius wilsonia*
__ Semipalmated Plover   *Charadrius semipalmatus*
__ Piping Plover   *Charadrius melodus*
__ Killdeer   *Charadrius vociferus*

Oystercatchers: (1 species)
__ American Oystercatcher   *Haematopus palliatus*

Stilts & Avocets: (2 species)
__ Black-necked Stilt   *Himantopus mexicanus*
__ American Avocet   *Recurvirostra americana*

Jacanas: (2 species)
__ Northern Jacana   *Jacana spinosa*
__ Wattled Jacana   *Jacana jacana*

Sandpipers and Allies: (29 species)
__ Spotted Sandpiper   *Actitis macularius*
__ Solitary Sandpiper   *Tringa solitaria*
__ Wandering Tattler   *Tringa incana*
__ Greater Yellowlegs   *Tringa melanoleuca*
__ Willet   *Tringa semipalmata*
__ Lesser Yellowlegs   *Tringa flavipes*
__ Upland Sandpiper   *Bartramia longicauda*
__ Whimbrel   *Numenius phaeopus*
__ Long-billed Curlew   *Numenius americanus*
__ Marbled Godwit   *Limosa fedoa*
__ Ruddy Turnstone   *Arenaria interpres*
__ Surfbird   *Aphriza virgata*
__ Red Knot   *Calidris canutus*
__ Sanderling   *Calidris alba*
__ Semipalmated Sandpiper   *Calidris pusilla*
__ Western Sandpiper   *Calidris mauri*
__ Least Sandpiper   *Calidris minutilla*
__ White-rumped Sandpiper   *Calidris fuscicollis*
__ Baird's Sandpiper   *Calidris bairdii*
__ Pectoral Sandpiper   *Calidris melanotos*
__ Dunlin   *Calidris alpina*
__ Stilt Sandpiper   *Calidris himantopus*
__ Buff-breasted Sandpiper   *Tryngites subruficollis*
__ Short-billed Dowitcher   *Limnodromus griseus*
__ Long-billed Dowitcher   *Limnodromus scolopaceus*
__ Wilson's Snipe   *Gallinago delicata*
__ Wilson's Phalarope   *Phalaropus tricolor*
__ Red-necked Phalarope   *Phalaropus lobatus*
__ Red Phalarope   *Phalaropus fulicarius*

Gulls, Terns and Skimmers: (23 species)

__ Sabine's Gull	*Xema sabini*
__ Laughing Gull	*Leucophaeus atricilla*
__ Franklin's Gull	*Leucophaeus pipixcan*
__ * Ring-billed Gull	*Larus delawarensis*
__ Herring Gull	*Larus argentatus*
__ * Lesser Black-backed Gull	*Larus fuscus*
__ * Kelp Gull	*Larus dominicanus*
__ Brown Noddy	*Anous stolidus*
__ Sooty Tern	*Onychoprion fuscatus*
__ Bridled Tern	*Onychoprion anaethetus*
__ Least Tern	*Sternula antillarum*
__ * Large-billed Tern	Phaelusa simplex
__ Gull-billed Tern	*Gelochelidon nilotica*
__ Caspian Tern	*Hydroprogne caspia*
__ Black Tern	*Childonias niger*
__ Roseate Tern	*Sterna dougallii*
__ Common Tern	*Sterna hirundo*
__ * Arctic Tern	*Sterna paradisaea*
__ Forster's Tern	*Sterna fosteri*
__ Royal Tern	*Thalasseus maximus*
__ Sandwich Tern	*Thalasseus sandvicensis*
__ Elegant Tern	*Thalasseus elegans*
__ Black Skimmer	*Rynchops niger*

Skuas and Jaegers: (3 species)

__ Pomarine Jaeger	*Stercorarius pomarinus*
__ Long-tailed Jaeger	*Stercorarius longicaudus*
__ Parasitic Jaeger	*Stercorarius parasiticus*

Pigeons & Doves: (21 species)

__ Rock Pigeon	*Columba livia*
__ Pale-vented Pigeon	*Patagioenas cayennensis*
__ Scaled Pigeon	*Patagioenas speciosa*
__ White-crowned Pigeon	*Patagioenas leucocephala*
__ Red-billed Pigeon	*Patagioenas flavirostris*
__ Band-tailed Pigeon	*Patagioenas fasciata*
__ Short-billed Pigeon	*Patagioenas nigrirostris*
__ White-winged Dove	*Zenaida asiatica*
__ Mourning Dove	*Zenaida macroura*

__ Inca Dove   *Columbina inca*
__ Common Ground-Dove   *Columbina passerina*
__ Plain-breasted Ground-Dove   *Columbina minuta*
__ Ruddy Ground-Dove   *Columbina talpacoti*
__ Blue Ground-Dove   *Claravis pretiosa*
__ White-tipped Dove   *Leptotila verreauxi*
__ Gray-headed Dove   *Leptotila plumbeiceps*
__ Gray-chested Dove   *Leptotila cassini*
__ Olive-backed Quail-Dove   *Geotrygon veraguensis*
__ White-faced Quail-Dove   *Geotrygon albifacies*
__ Violaceous Quail-Dove   *Geotrygon violacea*
__ Ruddy Quail-Dove   *Geotrygon montana*

Cuckoos and Anis: (11 species)
__ Squirrel Cuckoo   *Piaya cayana*
__ Yellow-billed Cuckoo   *Coccyzus americanus*
__ Mangrove Cuckoo   *Coccyzus minor*
__ Black-billed Cuckoo   *Coccyzus erythropthalmus*
__ Striped Cuckoo   *Tapera naevia*
__ Pheasant Cuckoo   *Dromococcyx phasianellus*
__ Lesser Ground-Cuckoo   *Moroccyx erthropygus*
__ Lesser Roadrunner   *Geococcyx velox*
__ Rufous-vented Ground-Cuckoo   *Neomorphus geoffroyi*
__ Smooth-billed Ani   *Crotophaga ani*
__ Groove-billed Ani   *Crotophaga sulcirostris*

Barn Owls: (1 species)
__ Barn Owl   *Tyto alba*

Owls and Pygmy Owls: (13 species)
__ Pacific Screech-Owl   *Megascops cooperi*
__ Whiskered Screech-Owl   *Megascops trichopsis*
__ Vermicualted Screech-Owl   *Megascops guatemalae*
__ Crested Owl   *Lophostrix cristata*
__ Spectacled Owl   *Pulsatrix perspicillata*
__ Great Horned Owl   *Bubo virginianus*
__ Northern Pygmy-Owl   *Glaucidium gnoma*
__ Central American Pygmy-Owl   *Glaucidium griseiceps*
__ Ferrugineous Pygmy-Owl   *Glaucidium brasilianum*
__ Mottled Owl   *Ciccaba virgata*
__ Black-and-White Owl   *Ciccaba nigrolineata*

__ Stygian Owl	*Asio stygius*
__ Striped Owl	*Pseudoscops clamator*

Nightjars: (11 species)

__ Short-tailed Nighthawk	*Lurocalis semitorquatus*
__ Lesser Nighthawk	*Chordeiles acutipennis*
__ Common Nighthawk	*Chordeiles minor*
__ Common Pauraque	*Nyctidromus albicollis*
__ Ocellated Poorwill	*Nyctiphrynus ocellatus*
__ Chuck-will's-widow	*Antrostomus carolinensis*
__ Tawny-collared Nightjar	*Antrostomus salvini*
__ Rufous Nightjar	*Antrostomus rufus*
__ Buff-collared Nightjar	*Antrostomus ridgwayi*
__ Eastern Whip-poor-will	*Antrostomus vociferus*
__ Spot-tailed Nightjar	*Caprimulgus maculicaudus*

Potoos: (3 species)

__ Great Potoo	*Nyctibius grandis*
__ Common Potoo	*Nyctibius griseus*
__ Northern Potoo	*Nyctibius jamaicensis*

Swifts: (9 species)

__ Black Swift	*Cypseloides niger*
__ White-chinned Swift	*Cypseloides cryptus*
__ Chestnut-collared Swift	*Streptoprocne rutila*
__ White-collared Swift	*Streptoprocne zonaris*
__ Chimney Swift	*Chaetura pelagica*
__ Vaux's Swift	*Chaetura vauxi*
__ Gray-rumped Swift	*Chaetura cinereiventris*
__ Lesser Swallow-tailed Swift	*Panyptila cayennensis*
__ Great Swallow-tailed Swift	*Panyptila sanctihieronymi*

Hummingbirds: (37 species)

__ White-necked Jacobin	*Florisuga mellivora*
__ Bronzy Hermit	*Glaucis aeneus*
__ Band-tailed Barbthroat	*Threnetes ruckeri*
__ Long-billed Hermit	*Phaethornis longirostris*
__ Little Hermit	*Phaethornis longuemareus*
__ Stripe-throated Hermit	*Phaethornis striigularis*
__ Brown Violetear	*Colibri delphinae*
__ Green Violetear	*Colibri thalassinus*

__ Purple-crowned Fairy   *Heliothryx barroti*
__ Green-breasted Mango   *Anthracothorax prevostii*
__ * Black-throated Mango   *Anthracothorax nigricollis*
__ Black-crested Coquette   *Lophornis helenae*
__ Magnificent Hummingbird *Eugenes fulgens*
__ Long-billed Starthroat   *Heliomaster longirostris*
__ Plain-capped Starthroat   *Heliomaster constantii*
__ Green-breasted Mountain-gem *Lampornis sybillae*
__ Purple-throated Mountain-gem *Lampornis calolaemus*
__ Sparkling-tailed Hummingbird *Tilmatura dupontii*
__ Ruby-throated Hummingbird *Archilochus colubris*
__ Canivet's Emerald   *Chlorostilbon canivetii*
__ Violet-headed Hummingbird *Klais guimeti*
__ Emerald-chinned Hummingbird *Abeillia abeillei*
__ Scaly-breasted Hummingbird *Phaeochroa cuvierii*
__ Violet Sabrewing   *Campylopterus hemileucurus*
__ Bronze-tailed Plumeleteer *Chalybura urochrysia*
__ Violet-crowned Woodnymph *Thalurania colombica*
__ Striped-tailed Hummingbird *Eupherusa eximia*
__ Snowcap   *Microchera albocoronata*
__ White-bellied Emerald   *Amazilia candida*
__ Blue-chested Hummingbird *Amazilia amabilis*
__ Azure-crowned Hummingbird *Amazilia cyanocephala*
__ Blue-tailed Hummingbird *Amazilia cyanura*
__ Steely-vented Hummingbird *Amazilia saucerrottei*
__ Rufous-tailed Hummingbird *Amazilia tzacatl*
__ Cinnamon Hummingbird *Amazilia rutila*
__ Blue-throated Goldentail *Hylocharis eliciae*
__ White-eared Hummingbird *Hylocharis leucotis*

Trogons: (8 species)
__ Resplendent Quetzal   *Pharomachrus mocinno*
__ Slaty-tailed Trogon   *Trogon massena*
__ Black-headed Trogon   *Trogon melanocephalus*
__ Gartered Trogon   *Trogon caligatus*
__ Black-throated Trogon   *Trogon rufus*
__ Elegant Trogon   *Trogon elegans*
__ Collared Trogon   *Trogon collaris*
__ Lattice-tailed Trogon   *Trogon calthratus*

Motmots: (6 species)
__ Tody Motmot   *Hylomanes momotula*
__ Blue-crowned Motmot   *Momotus coeruliceps*
__ Rufous Motmot   *Baryphthengus martii*
__ Keel-billed Motmot   *Electron carinatum*
__ Broad-billed Motmot   *Electron platyrhynchum*
__ Turquoise-browed Motmot   *Eumomota superciliosa*

Kingfishers: (6 species)
__ Ringed Kingfisher   *Megaceryl torquata*
__ Belted Kingfisher   *Megaceryl alcyon*
__ Amazon Kingfisher   *Choloceryle amazona*
__ Green Kingfisher   *Chloroceryle americana*
__ Green-and-Rufous Kingfisher   *Chloroceryle inda*
__ American Pygmy Kingfisher   *Chloroceryle aenea*

Puffbirds: (4 species)
__ White-necked Puffbird   *Notharchus hyperrhynchus*
__ Pied Puffbird   *Notharchus tectus*
__ White-whiskered Puffbird   *Malacoptila panamensis*
__ White-fronted Nunbird   *Monasa morphoeus*

Jacamars: (2 species)
__ Rufous-tailed Jacamar   *Galbula ruficauda*
__ Great Jacamar   *Jacamerops aureus*

Toucans: (5 species)
__ Emerald Toucanet   *Aulacorhynchus prasinus*
__ Collared Aracari   *Pteroglossus torquatus*
__ Yellow-eared Toucanet   *Selenidera spectabilis*
__ Black-mandibled Toucan   *Ramphastos ambiguus*
__ Keel-billed Toucan   *Ramphastos sulfuratus*

Woodpeckers: (16 species)
__ Olivaceous Piculet   *Picumnus olivaceus*
__ Acorn Woodpecker   *Melanerpes formicivorus*
__ Black-cheeked Woodpecker   *Melanerpes pucherani*
__ Hoffmann's Woodpecker   *Melanerpes hoffmannii*
__ Golden-fronted Woodpecker   *Melanerpes aurifrons*
__ Yellow-bellied Sapsucker   *Sphyrapicus varius*
__ Ladder-backed Woodpecker   *Picoides scalaris*

__ Smoky-brown Woodpecker	*Picoides fumigatus*
__ Hairy Woodpecker	*Picoides villosus*
__ Rufous-winged Woodpecker	*Piculus simplex*
__ Golden Olive Woodpecker	*Piculus rubiginosus*
__ Northern Flicker	*Colaptes auratus*
__ Cinnamon Woodpecker	*Celeus loricatus*
__ Chestnut-colored Woodpecker	*Celeus castaneus*
__ Lineated Woodpecker	*Dryocopus lineatus*
__ Pale-billed Woodpecker	*Campephilus guatemalensis*

Falcons & Caracaras: (13 species)

__ Barred Forest-Falcon	*Micrastur ruficollis*
__ * Slaty-backed Forest-Falcon	*Micrastur mirandollei*
__ Collared Forest-Falcon	*Micrastur semitorquatus*
__ Red-throated Caracara	*Ibycter americanus*
__ Crested Caracara	*Caracara cheriway*
__ Yellow-headed Caracara	*Milvago chimachima*
__ Laughing Falcon	*Herpetotheres cachinnans*
__ American Kestrel	*Falco sparverius*
__ Merlin	*Falco columbarius*
__ Aplomado Falcon	*Falco femoralis*
__ Bat Falcon	*Falco rufigularis*
__ Orange-breasted Falcon	*Falco deiroleucus*
__ Peregrine Falcon	*Falco peregrinus*

Parakeets & Parrots: (16 species)

__ Green Parakeet	*Aratinga holochlora*
__ Pacific Parakeet	*Aratinga strenua*
__ Crimson-fronted Parakeet	*Aratinga finschi*
__ Olive-throated Parakeet	*Aratinga nana*
__ Orange-fronted Parakeet	*Aratinga canicularis*
__ Great Green Macaw	*Ara ambiguus*
__ Scarlet Macaw	*Ara macao*
__ Barred Parakeet	*Bolborhynchus lineola*
__ Orange-chinned Parakeet	*Brotogeris jugularis*
__ Brown-hooded Parrot	*Pyrilia haematotis*
__ Blue-headed Parrot	*Pionus menstruus*
__ White-crowned Parrot	*Pionus senilis*
__ White-fronted Parrot	*Amazona albifrons*
__ Red-lored Parrot	*Amazona autumnalis*

__ Mealy Parrot   *Amazona farinosa*
__ Yellow-naped Parrot   *Amazona auropalliata*

Antbirds: (18 species)
__ Fasciated Antshrike   *Cymbilaimus lineatus*
__ Great Antshrike   *Taraba major*
__ Barred Antshrike   *Thamnophilus doliatus*
__ Western Slaty Antshrike   *Thamnophilus atrinucha*
__ Russet Antshrike   *Thamnistes anabatinus*
__ Plain Antvireo   *Dysithamnus mentalis*
__ Streak-crowned Antvireo   *Dysithamnus striaticeps*
__ Checker-throated Antwren   *Epinecrophylla fulviventris*
__ White-flanked Antwren   *Myrmotherula axillaris*
__ Slaty Antwren   *Myrmotherula schisticolor*
__ Dot-winged Antwren   *Microrhopias quixensis*
__ Dusky Antbird   *Cercomacra tyrannina*
__ Bare-crowned Antbird   *Gymnocichla nudiceps*
__ Chestnut-backed Antbird   *Myrmeciza exsul*
__ Wing-banded Antbird   *Myrmornis torquata*
__ Bicolored Antbird   *Gymnopithys leucaspis*
__ Spotted Antbird   *Hylophylax naevioides*
__ Ocellated Antbird   *Phaenostictus mcleannani*

Antpittas: (3 species)
__ Scaled Antpitta   *Grallaria guatimalensis*
__ Streak-chested Antpitta   *Hylopezus perspicillatus*
__ Thicket Antpitta   *Hylopezus dives*

Antthrushes: (1 species)
__ Black-faced Antthrush   *Formicarius analis*

Ovenbirds and Woodcreepers: (25 species)
__ Tawny-throated Leaftosser   *Sclerurus mexicanus*
__ Scaly-throated Leaftosser   *Sclerurus guatemalensis*
__ Olivaceous Woodcreeper   *Sittasomus griseicapillus*
__ Long-tailed Woodcreeper   *Deconychura longicauda*
__ Plain-brown Woodcreeper   *Dendrocincla fuliginosa*
__ Tawny-winged Woodcreeper   *Dendrocincla anabatina*
__ Ruddy Woodcreeper   *Dendrocincla homochroa*
__ Wedge-billed Woodcreeper   *Glyphorhynchus spirurus*
__ Northern Barred Woodcreeper   *Dendrocolaptes sanctithomae*

__ Black-banded Woodcreeper	*Dendrocolaptes picumnus*
__ Strong-billed Woodcreeper	*Xiphocolaptes romeropirhynchus*
__ Cocoa Woodcreeper	*Xiphorhynchus susurrans*
__ Ivory-billed Woodcreeper	*Xiphorhynchus flavigaster*
__ Black-striped Woodcreeper	*Xiphorhynchus lachrymosus*
__ Spotted Woodcreeper	*Xiphorhynchus erythropygius*
__ Brown-billed Scythebill	*Campylorhamphus pusillus*
__ Streaked-headed Woodcreeper	*Lepidocolaptes souleyetii*
__ Spot-crowned Woodcreeper	*Lepidocolaptes affinis*
__ Plain Xenops	*Xenops minutus*
__ Streaked Xenops	*Xenops rutilans*
__ Scaly-throated Foliage-gleaner	*Anabacerthia variegaticeps*
__ Striped Woodhaunter	*Hyloctistes subulatus*
__ Buff-throated Foliage-gleaner	*Automolus ochrolaemus*
__ Ruddy Foliage-gleaner	*Automolus rubiginosus*
__ Slaty Spinetail	*Synallaxis brachyura*

Tyrant Flycatchers: (65 species)

__ Yellow-bellied Tyrannulet	*Ornithion semiflavum*
__ Brown-capped Tyrannulet	*Ornithion brunneicapillus*
__ Northern Beardless-Tyrannulet	*Camptostoma imberbe*
__ Yellow Tyrannulet	*Capsiempis flaveola*
__ Greenish Elaenia	*Myiopagis viridicata*
__ Yellow-bellied Elaenia	*Elaenia flavogaster*
__ Mountain Elaenia	*Elaenia frantzii*
__ Ochre-bellied Flycatcher	*Mionectes oleagineus*
__ Sepia-capped Flycatcher	*Leptopogon amaurocephalus*
__ Paltry Tyrannulet	*Zimmerius vilissimus*
__ Black-capped Pygmy Tyrant	*Myiornis atricapillus*
__ Scale-crested Pygmy Tyrant	*Lophotriccus pileatus*
__ Northern Bentbill	*Oncostoma cinereigulare*
__ Slate-headed Tody-Flycatcher	*Poecilotriccus sylvia*
__ Black-headed Tody-Flycatcher	*Todirostrum nigriceps*
__ Common Tody-Flycatcher	*Todirostrum cinereum*
__ Eye-ringed Flatbill	*Rhynchocyclus brevirostris*
__ Yellow-olive Flycatcher	*Tolmomyias sulphurescens*
__ Yellow-margined Flycatcher	*Tolmomyias assimilis*
__ Stub-tailed Spadebill	*Platyrinchus cancrominus*
__ White-throated Spadebill	*Platyrinchus mystaceus*
__ Golden-crowned Spadebill	*Platyrinchus coranatus*

221

__	Royal Flycatcher	*Onychorhynchus coronatus*
__	Ruddy-tailed Flycatcher	*Terenotriccus erythrurus*
__	Sulphur-rumped Flycatcher	*Myiobius sulphureipygius*
__	Tawny-chested Flycatcher	*Aphanotriccus capitalis*
__	Tufted Flycatcher	*Mitrephanes phaeocercus*
__	Olive-sided Flycatcher	*Contopus cooperi*
__	Greater Pewee	*Contopus pertinax*
__	Western Wood-Pewee	*Contopus sordidulus*
__	Eastern Wood-Pewee	*Contopus virens*
__	Tropical Pewee	*Contopus cinereus*
__	Yellow-bellied Flycatcher	*Empidonax flaviventris*
__	Acadian Flycatcher	*Empidonax virescens*
__	Alder Flycatcher	*Empidonax alnorum*
__	Willow Flycatcher	*Empidonax traillii*
__	White-throated Flycatcher	*Empidonax albigularis*
__	Least Flycatcher	*Empidonax minimus*
__	Hammond's Flycatcher	*Empidonax hammondii*
__	Yellowish Flycatcher	*Empidonax flavescens*
__	Black Phoebe	*Sayornis nigricans*
__	Vermilion Flycatcher	*Pyrocephalus rubinus*
__	Long-tailed Tyrant	*Colonia colonus*
__	Bright-rumped Attila	*Attila spadiceus*
__	Rufous Mourner	*Rhytipterna holerythra*
__	Dusky-capped Flycatcher	*Myiarchus tuberculifer*
__	Ash-throated Flycatcher	*Myiarchus cinerascens*
__	Nutting's Flycatcher	*Myiarchus nuttingi*
__	Great Crested Flycatcher	*Myiarchus crinitus*
__	Brown-crested Flycatcher	*Myiarchus tyrannulus*
__	Great Kiskadee	*Pitangus sulphuratus*
__	Boat-billed Flycatcher	*Megarynchus pitangua*
__	Social Flycatcher	*Myiozetetes similis*
__	Gray-capped Flycatcher	*Myiozetetes granadensis*
__	White-ringed Flycatcher	*Conopias albovittatus*
__	Streaked Flycatcher	*Myiodynastes maculatus*
__	Sulphur-bellied Flycatcher	*Myiodynastes luteiventris*
__	Piratic Flycatcher	*Legatus leucophaius*
__	Tropical Kingbird	*Tyrannus melancholicus*
__	Cassin's Kingbird	*Tyrannus vociferans*
__	Western Kingbird	*Tyrannus verticalis*
__	Eastern Kingbird	*Tyrannus tyrannus*

__ Gray Kingbird	*Tyrannus dominicensis*
__ Scissor-tailed Flycatcher	*Tyrannus forficatus*
__ Fork-tailed Flycatcher	*Tyrannus savanna*

Cotinga: (6 species)

__ Purple-throated Fruitcrow	*Querula purpurata*
__ Bare-necked Umbrellabird	*Cephalopterus glabricollis*
__ Lovely Cotinga	*Cotinga amabilis*
__ Rufous Piha	*Lipaugus unirufus*
__ Three-wattled Bellbird	*Procnias tricarunculatus*
__ Snowy Cotinga	*Carpodectes nitidus*

Manakins: (6 species)

__ White-ruffed Manakin	*Corapipo altera*
__ White-collared Manakin	*Manacus candei*
__ Long-tailed Manakin	*Chiroxiphia linearis*
__ Blue-crowned Manakin	*Lepidothrix coronata*
__ Red-capped Manakin	*Pipra mentalis*
__ Gray-headed Piprites	*Piprites griseiceps*

Tityras and Allie: (8 species)

__ Black-crowned Tityra	*Tityra inquisitor*
__ Masked Tityra	*Tityra semifasciata*
__ Northern Shiffornis	*Schiffornis veraepacis*
__ Speckled Mourner	*Laniocera rufescens*
__ Cinnamon Becard	*Pachyramphus cinnamomeus*
__ White-winged Becard	*Pachyramphus polychopterus*
__ Gray-collared Becard	*Pachyramphus major*
__ Rose-throated Becard	*Pachyramphus aglaiae*

Vireos: (15 species)

__ White-eyed Vireo	*Vireo griseus*
__ Mangrove Vireo	*Vireo pallens*
__ Bell's Vireo	*Vireo bellii*
__ Yellow-throated Vireo	*Vireo flavifrons*
__ Blue-headed Vireo	*Vireo solitarius*
__ Warbling Vireo	*Vireo gilvus*
__ Brown-capped Vireo	*Vireo leucophrys*
__ Philadelphia Vireo	*Vireo philadelphicus*
__ Red-eyed Vireo	*Vireo olivaceus*
__ Yellow-green Vireo	*Vireo flavovirdis*

__ Scrub Greenlet   *Hylophilus flavipes*
__ Tawny-crowned Greenlet   *Hylophilus ochraceiceps*
__ Lesser Greenlet   *Hylophilus decurtatus*
__ Green Shike-Vireo   *Vireolanius pulchellus*
__ Rufous-browed Peppershrike   *Cyclarhis gujanensis*

Crows, Jays and Magpies: (6 species)
__ White-throated Magpie-Jay   *Calocitta formosa*
__ Brown Jay   *Psilorhinus morio*
__ Green Jay   *Cyanocorax yncas*
__ Bushy-crested Jay   *Cyanocorax melanocyaneus*
__ Steller's Jay   *Cyanocitta stelleri*
__ Common Raven   *Corvus corax*

Swallows: (12 species)
__ Blue-and-White Swallow   *Pygochelidon cyanoleuca*
__ Northern Rough-winged Swallow   *Stelgidopteryx serripennis*
__ Southern Rough-winged Swallow   *Stelgidopteryx ruficollis*
__ Purple Martin   *Progne subis*
__ Gray-breasted Martin   *Progne chalybea*
__ Tree Swallow   *Tachycineta bicolor*
__ Mangrove Swallow   *Tachycineta albilinea*
__ Violet-green Swallow   *Tachycineta thalassina*
__ Bank Swallow   *Riparia riparia*
__ Barn Swallow   *Hirundo rustica*
__ Cliff Swallow   *Petrochelidon pyrrhonota*
__ Cave Swallow   *Petrochelidon fulva*

Treecreepers: (1 species)
__ Brown Creeper   *Certhia americana*

Wrens: (18 species)
__ Rock Wren   *Salpinctes obsoletus*
__ Nightingale Wren   *Microcerculus philomela*
__ House Wren   *Troglodytes aedon*
__ Rufous-browed Wren   *Troglodytes ruficiliatus*
__ Sedge Wren   *Cistothorus platensis*
__ Carolina Wren   *Thryothorus ludovicianus*
__ Banded-backed Wren   *Campylorhynchus zonatus*
__ Rufous-naped Wren   *Campylorhynchus rufinucha*
__ Spot-breasted Wren   *Pheugopedius maculipectus*

___ Black-throated Wren   *Pheugopedius atrogularis*
___ Banded Wren   *Thryophilus pleurostictus*
___ Rufous-and-white Wren   *Thryophilus rufalbus*
___ Stripe-breasted Wren   *Cantorchilus thoracicus*
___ Plain Wren   *Cantorchilus modestus*
___ Bay Wren   *Cantorchilus nigricapillus*
___ White-breasted Wood-Wren   *Henicorhina leucosticta*
___ Gray-breasted Wood-Wren   *Henicorhina leucophrys*
___ Song Wren   *Cyphorhunis phaeocephalus*

Gnatcatchers: (5 species)
___ Tawny-faced Gnatwren   *Microbates cinereiventris*
___ Long-billed Gnatwren   *Ramphocaenus melanurus*
___ Blue-gray Gnatcatcher   *Polioptila caerulea*
___ White-lored Gnatcatcher   *Polioptila albiloris*
___ Tropical Gratcatcher   *Polioptila plumbea*

Dippers: (1 species)
___ American Dipper   *Cinclus mexicanus*

Thrushes and Allies: (14 species)
___ Eastern Bluebird   *Sialia sialis*
___ Slate-colored Solitaire   *Myadestes unicolor*
___ Orange-billed Nightingale-Thrush *Catharus aurantiirostris*
___ Ruddy-capped Nightingale-Thrush *Catharus frantzii*
___ Black-headed Nightingale-Thrush *Catharus mexicanus*
___ Spotted Nightingale-Thrush   *Catharus dryas*
___ Veery   *Catharus fuscescens*
___ Gray-cheeked Thrush   *Catharus minimus*
___ Swainson's Thrush   *Catharus ustulatus*
___ Wood Thrush   *Hylocichla mustelina*
___ Black Thrush   *Turdus infuscatus*
___ Mountain Thrush   *Turdus plebejus*
___ Clay-colored Thrush   *Turdus grayi*
___ White-throated Thrush   *Turdus assimilis*

Mockingbirds and Thrashers: (3 species)
___ Gray Catbird   *Dumetella carolinensis*
___ Tropical Mockingbird   *Mimus gilvus*
___ Blue-and-white Mockingbird   *Melanotis hypoleucus*

Waxwings: (1 species)
__ Cedar Waxwing   *Bombycilla cedrorum*

Olive Warbler: (1 species)
__ Olive Warbler   *Peucedramus taeniatus*

Wood Warblers: (47 species)
__ Ovenbird   *Seiurus aurocapilla*
__ Worm-eating Warbler   *Helmitheros vermivorum*
__ Louisiana Waterthrush   *Parkesia motacilla*
__ Northern Waterthrush   *Parkesia noveboracensis*
__ Blue-winged Warbler   *Vermivora cyanoptera*
__ Golden-winged Warbler   *Vermivora chrysoptera*
__ Black-and-white Warbler   *Mniotilta varia*
__ Prothonotary Warbler   *Protonotaria citrea*
__ Crescent-chested Warbler   *Oreothlypis superciliosa*
__ Tennessee Warbler   *Oreothlypis peregrina*
__ Gray-crowned Yellowthroat   *Geothlypis poliocephala*
__ MacGillivray's Warbler   *Geothlypis tolmiei*
__ Mourning Warbler   *Geothlypis philadelphia*
__ Kentucky Warbler   *Geothlypis formosus*
__ Olive-crowned Yellowthroat   *Geothlypis semiflava*
__ Common Yellowthroat   *Geothlypis trichas*
__ Hooded Warbler   *Setophaga citrina*
__ American Redstart   *Setophaga ruticilla*
__ Cape May Warbler   *Setophaga tigrina*
__ Cerulean Warbler   *Setophaga cerulea*
__ Northern Parula   *Setophaga americana*
__ Tropical Parula   *Setophaga pitiayumi*
__ Magnolia Warbler   *Setophaga magnolia*
__ Bay-breasted Warbler   *Setophaga castanea*
__ Blackburnian Warbler   *Setophaga fusca*
__ Yellow Warbler   *Setophaga petechia*
__ Chestnut-sided Warbler   *Setophaga pensylvanica*
__ Blackpoll Warbler   *Setophaga striata*
__ Black-throated Blue Warbler   *Setophaga caerulescens*
__ Palm Warbler   *Setophaga palmarum*
__ Yellow-rumped Warbler   *Setophaga coronata*
__ Yellow-throated Warbler   *Setophaga dominica*
__ Prairie Warbler   *Setophaga discolor*

__ Grace's Warbler	*Setophaga graciae*
__ Townsend's Warbler	*Setophaga townsendi*
__ Hermit Warbler	*Setophaga occidentalis*
__ Golden-cheeked Warbler	*Setophaga chrysoparia*
__ Black-throated Green Warbler	*Setophaga virens*
__ Fan-tailed Warbler	*Basileuterus lachrymosa*
__ Rufous-capped Warbler	*Basileuterus rufifrons*
__ Golden-crowned Warbler	*Basileuterus culicivorus*
__ Buff-rumped Warbler	*Myiothlypis fulvicauda*
__ Canada Warbler	*Cardelina canadensis*
__ Wilson's Warbler	*Cardelina pusilla*
__ Painted Redstart	*Myioborus pictus*
__ Slate-throated Redstart	*Myioborus miniatus*
__ Yellow-breasted Chat	*Icteria virens*

Tanagers and Allies: (37 species)

__ Gray-headed Tanager	*Eucometis penicillata*
__ White-shouldered Tanager	*Tachyphonus luctuosus*
__ Tawny-crested Tanager	*Tachyphonus delatrii*
__ White-lined Tanager	*Tachyphonus rufus*
__ White-throated Shrike-Tanager	*Lanio leucothorax*
__ Crimson-collared Tanager	*Ramphocelus sanguinolentus*
__ Passerini's Tanager	*Ramphocelus passerinii*
__ Blue-gray Tanager	*Thraupis episcopus*
__ Yellow-winged Tanager	*Thraupis abbas*
__ Palm Tanager	*Thraupis palmarum*
__ Golden-hooded Tanager	*Tangara larvata*
__ Plain-colored Tanager	*Tangara inornata*
__ Rufous-winged Tanager	*Tangara lavinia*
__ Bay-headed Tanager	*Tangara gyrola*
__ Scarlet-thighed Dacnis	*Dacnis venusta*
__ Blue Dacnis	*Dacnis cayana*
__ Shining Honeycreeper	*Cyanerpes lucidus*
__ Red-legged Honeycreeper	*Cyanerpes cyaneus*
__ Green Honeycreeper	*Chlorophanes spiza*
__ Cinnamon-bellied Flowerpiercer	*Diglossa baritula*
__ Slaty Finch	*Haplospiza rustica*
__ Grassland Yellow-Finch	*Sicalis luteola*
__ Blue-black Grassquit	*Volatina jacarina*
__ Slate-colored Seedeater	*Sporophila schistacea*

__ Variable Seedeater   *Sporophila corvina*
__ White-collared Seedeater   *Sporophila torqueola*
__ Yellow-bellied Seedeater   *Sporophila nigricollis*
__ Ruddy-breasted Seedeater   *Sporophila minuta*
__ Nicaraguan Seed-Finch   *Oryzoborus nuttingi*
__ Thick-billed Seed-Finch   *Oryzoborus funereus*
__ Bananaquit   *Coereba flaveola*
__ Yellow-faced Grassquit   *Tiaris olivaceus*
__ Dusky-faced Tanager   *Mitrospingus cassinii*
__ Grayish Saltator   *Saltator coerulescens*
__ Buff-throated Saltator   *Saltator maximus*
__ Black-headed Saltator   *Saltator atriceps*
__ Slate-colored Grosbeak   *Saltator grossus*

Buntings and New World Sparrows: (13 species)
__ Chestnut-capped Brush-Finch   *Arremon brunneinucha*
__ Orange-billed Sparrow   *Arremon aurantiirostris*
__ Olive Sparrow   *Arremonops rufivirgatus*
__ Black-striped Sparrow   *Arremonops conirostris*
__ White-naped Brush-Finch   *Atlapetes albinucha*
__ Rusty Sparrow   *Aimophila rufescens*
__ White-eared Ground-Sparrow   *Melozone leucotis*
__ Stripe-headed Sparrow   *Peucaea ruficauda*
__ Botteri's Sparrow   *Peucaea bottterii*
__ Chipping Sparrow   *Spizella passerina*
__ Grasshopper Sparrow   *Ammodramus savannarum*
__ Rufous-collared Sparrow   *Zonotrichia capensis*
__ Common Bush-Tanager   *Chlorospingus ophthalmicus*

Cardinals and Allies: (18 species)
__ Hepatic Tanager   *Piranga flava*
__ Summer Tanager   *Piranga rubra*
__ Scarlet Tanager   *Piranga olivacea*
__ Western Tanager   *Piranga ludoviciana*
__ Flame-colored Tanager   *Piranga bidentata*
__ White-winged Tanager   *Piranga leucoptera*
__ Red-crowned Ant-Tanager   *Habia rubica*
__ Red-throated Ant-Tanager   *Habia fuscicauda*
__ Carmiol's Tanager   *Chlorothraupis carmioli*
__ Black-faced Grosbeak   *Caryothraustes poliogaster*
__ Rose-breasted Grosbeak   *Pheucticus ludovicianus*

__ Blue Seedeater	*Amaurospiza concolor*
__ Blue-black Grosbeak	*Cyanocompsa cyaniodes*
__ Blue Bunting	*Cyanocompsa parellina*
__ Blue Grosbeak	*Passerina caerulea*
__ Indigo Bunting	*Passerina cyanea*
__ Painted Bunting	*Passerina ciris*
__ Dickcissel	*Spiza americana*

Blackbirds: (23 species)

__ Bobolink	*Dolichonyx oryzivorus*
__ Red-winged Blackbird	*Agelaius phoeniceus*
__ * Red-breasted Blackbird	*Sturnella militaris*
__ Eastern Meadowlark	*Sturnella magna*
__ Yellow-headed Blackbird	*Xanthocephalus xanthocephalus*
__ Melodious Blackbird	*Dives dives*
__ Great-tailed Grackle	*Quiscalus mexicanus*
__ Nicaraguan Grackle	*Quiscalus nicaraguensis*
__ Bronzed Cowbird	*Molothrus aeneus*
__ Giant Cowbird	*Molothrus oryzivorus*
__ Black-vented Oriole	*Icterus wagleri*
__ Black-cowled Oriole	*Icterus prosthemelas*
__ Orchard Oriole	*Icterus spurius*
__ Yellow-backed Oriole	*Icterus chrysater*
__ Yellow-tailed Oriole	*Icterus mesomelas*
__ Streak-backed Oriole	*Icterus pustulatus*
__ Spot-breasted Oriole	*Icterus pectoralis*
__ Altamira Oriole	*Icterus gularis*
__ Baltimore Oriole	*Icterus galbula*
__ Yellow-billed Cacique	*Amblycercus holosericeus*
__ Scarlet-rumped Cacique	*Cacicus uropygialis*
__ Chestnut-headed Oropendola	*Psarocolius wagleri*
__ Montezuma Oropendola	*Psarocolius montezuma*

Siskins, Crossbills and Allies: (11 species)

__ Scrub Euphonia	*Euphonia affinis*
__ Yellow-crowned Euphonia	*Euphonia luteicapilla*
__ Yellow-throated Euphonia	*Euphonia hirundinacea*
__ Elegant Euphonia	*Euphonia elegantissima*
__ Olive-backed Euphonia	*Euphonia gouldi*
__ White-vented Euphonia	*Euphonia minuta*

__ Blue-crowned Chlorophonia   *Chlorophonia occipitalis*
__ Golden-browed Chlorophonia   *Chlorophonia callophrys*
__ Red Crossbill   *Loxia curvirostra*
__ Black-headed Siskin   *Spinus notata*
__ Lesser Goldfinch   *Spinus psaltria*

Old World Sparrows: (1 species)
__ House Sparrow   *Passer domesticus*

References

The information for the various birding sites contained in this book was derived from a wide range of sources, including interviews with the owners and staff at various reserves. The maps and bird lists were generously provided by the reserves as well as my colleagues Jose Manuel Zolotoff and Salvadora Morales. Other sources include brochures and publications produced for the many reserves and a range of websites.

Arendt, Wayne and Marvin A. Tórrez. 2013. First record of Arctic Tern *Sterna paradisaea* for Nicaragua. Journal NBC, Cotinga 35: 79–81.

Batchelder, Robert L. and Klemens Steiof. 2013. Second record of Ocellated Poorwill Nyctiphrymas ocelatus for Nicaragua and third record for Costa Rica. Journal NBC, Cotinga 34: 90–91.

Chavarría, Liliana & Georges Duriaux. 2013 Estado del Hormiguero Alifranjeado *Myrmornis torquata* (Status of the Wing-banded Antbird) en Nicaragua. Cotinga 35: 69–73.

Garrigues, Richard and Robert Dean. 2007. The Birds of Costa Rica. Zona Tropical, Cornell Univeristy, Ithica, NY.

Hernandez, Sandra, Salvadora Morales, Wayne Arendt, Marvin Torres. 2009. Bird Checklist Cerro Datanli-El Diablo Nature Reserve, Nicaragua. Managua, Jerry Bauer, 2009, 55p.

Howell, Steve & Sophie Webb. 1995. A Guide to the Birds of Mexico and Northern Central America, Oxford University Press.

Lola, Carlos R. 2008. The Masaya Volcano National Park. Managua, Nicaragua.

Martínez Sánchez, J. C. and T. Will. 2010. Thomas R. Howell's Checklist of the Birds of Nicaragua as of 1993. Ornithological Monographs, No. 68.

Martinez-Sanchez, J.C. 2007. Lista Patron de Las Aves de Nicargua. (includes 708 species). Alianza para las Areas Silvestres (ALAS), Managua, Nicaragua.

Martinez-Sanchez, J.C. 2000. Lista Patron de Las Aves de Nicargua. (includes 650 species). Fundacion Cocibolca, Managua.

Martínez Sánchez, Juan Carlos & Alejandra Martinex, Jose Manuel Zolotoff, M. Lezama. Checklist of Birds at La Reserva Silvestre Privada Domitila.

McCrary, Jeff & Wayne Arendt, Salvadora Morales, T. Arengi and Lorenzo Lopez. 2001. New avian sight records for Nicaragua, with notes on abundance, distribution and habitat use. Journal of the Neotropical Bird Club, Cotinga 29.

Morales, Salvadora & Jose Manuel Zolotoff, Mariamar Gutierrez & Marvin Torrez. 2009. Important Bird Areas Americas—Nicaragua, Bird Life International.

Morales, Salvadora, Diego Osorno, Wayne J. Arendt and Sandra Hernandez. 2008. Bird Checklist Ometepe Island, Nicaragua. Managua. 40 p.

Munera-Roldan, Claudia & Martin Cody, Robin Schiele-Zavala, Bryan Sigel, Stefan Woltmann, Jorgen Kjeldsen. 2007. New and noteworthy records of birds from south-eastern Nicaragua, Bull. B.O.C. 127(2), p.152 161.

Ridgely, Robert & John Gwynne. 1989. A Guide to the Birds of Panama, with Costa Rica, Nicaragua and Honduras, Princeton University Press.

Salmeron Belli, Pomares & Wayne Arendt. Bird Checlist Montibelli Private Wildlife Reserve, Nicaragua. U.S. Forest Service. 38p.

Sandoval, Luis & Wayne Arendt. 2010. Two new species for Nicaragua and other notes on the avifauna of the Atlantic Region and Paso del Istmo Biological Corridor. Journal of NBC, Cotinga no. 33, p 50–57.

Stiles, Gary & Alexander Skutch. 1989. Guide to the Birds of Costa Rica. Cornell University, Ithica, NY.

Streifert, Kristi. 2006. A Nicaraguan Sampler. Winging It, Newsletter of the American Birding Association, Sept/Oct. p. 3–5.

Sullivan, B.L., C.L. Wood, M.J. Iliff, R.E. Bonney, D. Fink, and S. Kelling. 2009. eBird: a citizen-based bird observation network in the biological sciences. Biological Conservation 142: 2282–2292.

Taylor, B.W. 1963. An Outline of the Vegetation of Nicaragua. The Journal of Ecology, vol 51, No 1, p 27–54.

Volkert, William & Susan Gilchrist. 2005. Nicaragua Project for Bird Conservation Education. Passenger Pigeon, vol 67, no 1.

Wiedenfield, David A. & Jose Morales and Marin Lezama. 2001. Sight records of new species for Nicaragua and noteworthy records on range and occurrence. Journal of the Neotropical Bird Club, Cotinga no. 15.

Zolotoff, Jose M & Juan Carlos Martinez-Sanchez. 2010. Areas Importantes Para la Observacion de Aves en Nicaragua (unpublished).

Zolotoff, Jose M, Marvin Torres, Mariamar Gutierrez and Salvadora Morales. 2006. Important Bird Areas (Areas Importantes para Aves) en Nicaragua. Unpublished report, Fundacion Cocibolca and Alianza par alas Aves, Managua. 88p.

Zolotoff-Pallais, Jose Manel, Mariamar Gutierrez Ramierez, Wayne Arendt and Alexander Acosta Anton. 2009. Bird Checklist Mombacho Volcano Nature Reserve and Adjacent Lowlands, Nicaragua. Managua, Jeffy Bauer, 59 p.

Unpublished Checklists:

Lista de Aves Reportadas en la Reserva Silvestre Privada Montibelli

Alianza para las Areas Silvestres (ALAS), Managua, Nicaragua.

Lista de Aves Reportadas en la Reserva Silvestre Privada El Jaguar

Alianza para las Areas Silvestres (ALAS), Managua, Nicaragua.

Lista de Aves Reportadas en la Reserva Silvestre Privada Esperanza Verde, Alianza para las Areas Silvestres (ALAS), Managua, Nicaragua.

Useful Websites:

www.avesnicaragua.org – for information and guides
www.nicabirds.com
www.vianica.com
http://www.visitanicaragua.com/
http://www.vianica.com/go/specials/9-nicaragua-volcanoes.html
http://www.vianica.com/visit/granada
http://www.vianica.com/visit/jinotega
http://www.vianica.com/animalguide.php
http://www.centralamerica.com/nigaragua/parks/nationalpark.htm
http://www.rainforestpublications.com/nicaragua-field-
    guides/index.html
Ramsar Convention—ramsar.org
Birdlife Interational—www.birdlife.org
Bird Songs and Calls—www.xeno-canto.org

Websites of Reserves by Region:

Pacific Lowlands

Masaya Volcano National Park
http://vianica.com/attraction/2/masaya-volcano-national-park.

Chocoyero Reserve	www.chocoyero.com
Montibelli Reserve	www.montibelli.com
Lake Apoyo	www.gaianicaragua.org.
Mombacho Volcano	www.mombacho.org www.mombotour.com

Pacific Coast

Chacocente Reserve	www.chacocente-nicaragua.com

Southern-Central

Los Guatuzos Reserve   www.fundar.org.ni
www.losguatuzos.com
www.nicaraguafishing.com
www.riosanjuan.info

Indio Maiz Reserve
Bartola Lodge   www.refugiobartola.com
Sabalos Lodge   www.sabaloslodge.com

Atlantic Lowlands

Rio Indio Lodge   www.therioindiolodge.com
Greenfields Reserve   www.greenfields.com.ni

Northern Highlands

Selva Negra Reserve   www.selvanegra.com
Cerro Datanli Reserve
La Bastilla Lodge   www.bastillaecolodge.com
El Jaguar Reserve   www.jaguarreserve.org
Mifaflor Reserve   www.miraflor.org
www.naturereservemiraflor.com

About the Author

Bill Volkert worked as the naturalist and wildlife educator for the Wisconsin Department of Natural Resources at Horicon Marsh for 27 years, where he conducted more than 3,600 education programs for over 220,000 people. His broad audiences include 66 delegations of scientists from 43 foreign countries who came for professional training. His work experience includes assisting experts from the Russian Natural Resources Agency and their Academy of Sciences to further protection of Lake Baikal, located in Siberia, Russia. From 1991 to 2004 he made 8 trips to the Republic of Buryatia and two trips to Mongolia. Since 2002, he has worked with ornithologists and environmental educators to help develop a National Bird Conservation Education Plan for Nicaragua and continues to support bird conservation projects in the country.

Bill Volkert

In his personal time he has traveled widely in search of the world's birds and the wild places they inhabit. His travels have taken him throughout Central and South America, across the Canadian Arctic, to Africa, Australia, New Zealand, Russia and Mongolia. Bill has been watching and studying birds for nearly 40 years and in his travels has sighted more than 2,500 species (1/4 of the world's birds). To facilitate his studies he is also a federally licensed master bird bander, in cooperation with the Bird Banding Laboratory of the U.S. Geological Survey.

Bill and his wife Connie make their home in the northern Kettle Moraine area of east-central Wisconsin. Here they work together to restore a series of native plant communities. On this land, they have now identified more than 600 species of plants and animals, including 203 species of birds.

Bill shares his experiences and understanding of the natural world through lectures, presentations, and field trips. He is also working on several writing projects that will give these presentations more permanence and reach an even wider public.

For more information see: www.billvolkert.com.

Orange-chinned Parakeet

Index

239